The Working Persons Pocket Guide to Boss And Employee Relations or

103 Ways to Leave Your Boss Speechless

By

Peter Shelton

This book is a work of non-fiction. Names and places have been changed to protect the privacy of all individuals. The events and situations are true.

ISBN: 1-4107-5945-8 (e-book)
ISBN: 1-4107-5944-X (Paperback)
ISBN: 1-4107-5943-1 (Dust Jacket)

This book is printed on acid free paper.

1stBooks – rev. 05/20/03

I want to thank my wife, Casey, without who I would never have finished this book. I also want to thank the people I had the honor to work with (no last names). Here they are: Rich, JR, Ron and Ron, Don, Chris, Mike. My friends, my co-workers, and people: I would have pulled out my hair if they weren't around. Thanks to those friends without who this would have never been possible Peter J Shelton.

I also want to thank Rebecca for proof reading this book who without her help this book would never happen. Thanks Rebecca.

-Author's note-

All of the names have been changed so they can't hunt me down.
All of this is 100% truth; just ask my wife

Here is an explanation of this book. This is not to downgrade
all managers, but to understand and fight back against bosses. At the
same time it is an explanation of the deterition of workers' rights over
the years. They are a whole other type of creation. These demi-god tin
dictators are the kind that try to beat you down with insults,
accusations, and stupid questions. A real manager does not have to.
They got to where they are by hard work, insight, and foresight and
not backstabbing, short-sightedness, or waiting for someone to die to
advance themselves. Managers are people who can understand what it
is like to be in your shoes and how hard you do work. A boss doesn't
care about hard work, just bottom line profits (even though you are
helping make it for them). They walk around trying to impress
everyone but always fall short.

A manager who I respect has the hardest job. They must keep
every one happy and at the same time have production. They also
must have tremendous patience, and try to do all of this with a cool
head and calm disposition. They don't need to ask you what you are
doing; they know. A boss, on the other hand, just wants to flex their
corporate muscles and throw the fear of God into you. A good boss
and a good owner don't need to prove to anyone that they are in
charge.

Anyway, that's it. I just wanted to let you know ahead of time.
I'm not disrespectful of managers and owners, just bosses who try to
control you with fear and humiliation. So we will poke fun at them
for awhile. Let's face it, we have all had them at one point or another
and have all been in these situations. Read on, and remember, it's all
truly in good fun.

Pete

Table of Contents

Introduction

This is not your everyday kind of book. This is a "get your boss off your back with quick wit and finesse" kind of book. This is the kind of book that every working stiff, male or female, shouldn't be without. It will tell you how to get your boss off your back and some funny insights along the way. I have had 22 different jobs and bosses and have seen all types. Now don't get me wrong. I was not fired from these jobs because of my work or my attitude, but when you realize your boss's intelligence is limited to, "I know what I'm doing," as he pushes a pull door even when it is clearly marked PULL, and under his breath he says, "Damn this door is stuck again," you may be like me and be ready to move on to greener pastures and a place that is not so DIM.

Oh, did I mention that this is not a boss-bashing book? It's just aimed to the ones who are deserving of it. I can tell you that a boss and a manager are two different things. A Boss, who we will be looking at in this book, is 9 times out of 10 a moron; a manager is a person who can get the work done without screaming, insults, or degrading people. Well you get the idea. Owners are the same way. They are not left out either. I have known great owners of companies and then there were the other types (you know, the morons). The ones in this book are, you guessed it, the morons. To the other types, the managers, owners, and CEOs, who are thinking people who not only care about making money but to be a decent person, this book is also dedicated to you. Hats off to you all. We need more of you. The workplace is filled with the other types with such wise questions like, "What are you doing?" even though they haven't got enough brain power to actually LOOK to see what you are doing. They would rather bother you while you are trying to do something to ask you mindless questions.

In this book I will be telling you some of the experiences that I have had and that of some of my friends as well as my wonderful wife (without her support and encouragement this book would not have gotten this far). (This is to keep me in good with her for all those long hours I was playing on the computer) hahaha

When I first started working, I was just 15 years old, and unfortunately for this book, my first boss was a good lady and was not a boss at all. She was a manager. So I was spoiled right off the bat. I knew how a good manager should act, and all who followed can't hold a candle to her. But the good news is the very next one was a true dolt. I worked at a grocery store for a short time. My boss had me doing all kinds of strange things. He got himself cut really badly once because he wanted to wash the light bulbs on the outside fixtures. Yes, I said wash the light bulbs on the outside fixtures. They were fluorescent, nice and safe, right? I was told to do it. I told him he was out of his tree. He wanted to show me just how safe they were. He took a rag and proceeded to wipe down the florescent bulb. (Instead of just putting new ones he ordered in that we got from the main store. He wanted to save those until they went bad.) Well, to make a long story short, when the bulb popped, he went to the hospital with 32 stitches in his wrist and a type of poison (that makes the light work) coursing thought his blood. Needless to say, the next day I put the new one in and never again was asked to wash down light bulbs.

This is just one example of the kind of ways some melon-heads want to save money and show a better bottom line. The book is filled with stories of such bosses with the "Higher learning" which got them their jobs. It has never stopped to amaze me that someone with the intelligence that some of these people have lack common sense. Corporate, it seems like, has even less of a clue than even most of the nitwits I have had the displeasure of working with. They don't want to order stock to fill the shelves but give some kind of discount for not having it in stock. They say, "Well, if we don't have it in stock, you can get a rain check for it at 30% off." They then pull the bonehead move of the year. They bitch because their overhead and/or cost are up! Well, duh! We blue-collar people may not always be the most educated ones in the group, but we are certainly smarter than someone trying to sell something they don't have, or who won't order the product because they are trying to keep overhead down, then turn around and give out discounts on sale merchandise they don't have yet because they didn't order it. Then we really lose money. But as we all know, for we have all seen it happen time and time again, "the bus driver knows best."

A lot of people also wonder what went on behind closed doors. I have seen and heard what happens. They say we beat time. HA! It is just a way to throw their weight and make everyone nervous about their jobs, and who they can fire to make the bottom line look better and still not lose production.

They didn't like my idea of getting rid of 1 of the 17 bosses they had at one time. We had more bosses than workers – two bosses for every one, NO waiting!

So needless to say, my idea was right. We couldn't have that (it made sense). I was told we needed all we have, and of course, I asked why? "To keep the work going" was told to me. Well I should have not said a word, but of course, I did. I implied does this mean you are coming out here to do some REAL WORK? That was my last meeting. It's funny; these bosses, not managers, want and ask your opinion, but when you give them an answer they don't like, they proceed to take their ball and go home. We poor working stiffs are the ones that have an attitude, or so we are told. The ones I like the most are the screamers. They make me laugh. I have more fun with them than any other boss type. I had one that always yelled at the top of his lungs at everyone about every thing. One fellow we worked with had this screamer figured out. The screamer would yell at him from across the room, "PICK IT UP! YOU'RE MOVING TOO SLOW!" Well, he said, "What? I can't hear ya." So the screamer would yell again, "GET IT MOVING!" This guy would just shake his head and walk over to him. It didn't matter if it was 10 feet or 100 feet and walk slowly and say, "I'm sorry. I didn't hear ya." The screamer never got it, and this fellow did that every time. Now don't get me wrong. We worked our tails off. We just didn't like to be yelled at like dogs. What made it even more humorous was that he never got it. One time he lost his voice, and we all did what we had seen this fellow do. He then went into what we commonly call a "duck fit." He figured out what he was doing and what we were doing and started laughing with us all.

This book is also to him. He became a decent manager when he found out that old saying is right: "You can get more flies with honey than you can with vinegar." We don't ask for much in the blue-collar class, just respect and not to be treated like we are lower class people because we like to work with our hands. That's why I don't take it anymore and why (as you'll see) I fight back and wrote this book. As I look back, I can't believe just how dumb some of this was and at least now I am getting a good laugh about it all.

Chapter 1

What are you doing?

This question has dumbfounded the mind of employees forever. Let's face it: we have all been guilty of staring into space for a minute or two, either gathering our thoughts or the big question, what's for dinner? There is always someone at the right place to ask you this stupid question. Most of the time they know what you're doing; they just want to let you know they're watching you. (Yeah, Yeah) So what? I have a few ways of giving them answers which will make you "either the life of the building or unemployed," but it will be fun either way it goes.

(All answers to be given with a straight face and an enlightening tone of voice)

"What are you doing?"

Answers:

1) Looking to God for answers.
2) I'm thinking of how to do my job more efficiently… Sir.
3) (Yawn & stretch) I'm sorry, what?
4) Being bored to tears.
5) I thought I was working until you interrupted me, and now I've lost my train of thought.
6) Praying I win the lottery.
7) Screwing off, why? (Then in turn, he will say, "well that is obvious." Your reply should be, "then why did you ask?")
8) Trying to remember to whom I last sent my resume.
9) I think I'm missing cartoons for this.
10) Working more and getting paid less.
11) Working more and enjoying it less.
12) Not a thing and getting paid for it. Thank you, Sir.
13) Writing a book about bosses (they will never believe this one)

1

14) HA HA! "That's a good one, sir," and walk away.
15) It's 3:00 PM. Why do you ask? This will confuse them.

What's bad about it is that out of this question will spawn a number of other questions that should never be asked by an intelligent person, but as you know, they do anyway.

"Are you busy?"

What's bad about most of these mouth-breathers is they don't even know what they are saying or how stupid it is (until you point it out to them). They ask this one at the most inopportune times. You are debugging a program on your computer, and your fax is going off. You have two phone calls (company business mind you), and this person is standing in your doorway asking, "Are you busy?" Even though you try to be polite, he still won't leave you alone, and continues to bombard you with other questions. I have never understood this one. Any idiot can see you are, but whatever it is this person wants is more important than what the other 17 Bosses want. So STOP what you are doing, and answer this person. If you say, "YES, I am busy," you're in trouble. They can say one or two things: "Well can you squeeze this in" or the best one is, "Well, how busy are you?"

You just want to scream and kick them. It would not matter what you were doing or how much you had to do, they still can't see that you're doing anything and think you should have more work to do. After all, idle hands are the devil's workshop, right?
Sorry, but I believe in a good hard day's work, but there comes a point where enough is enough. I am not a robot. A boss once told me that a good employee skips lunch and works until the work is done, whether it is an 8 hour day or a 16 hour day. Just because I only worked 10 and 12 hour days, I was not a dedicated employee. I said, "sorry I have a life, and it does not revolve around my job." What people in the boss's circle don't understand is that a job is a means to an end. It is a way to have a family. The bosses and the government always bitch about family values, but how can you teach this if you

2

and your spouse are not home to do it? It went right over his head. I was again told that I was not dedicated. Oh, well, trying to talk intelligently to a boss is like debating quantum theory with a brick.

So the "are you busy" question really confuses me. I mean what does he think you are going to say? "No, not at all. Go ahead and fire me. Someone else can do all this." One time I had a manager who asked me this, and instead of me even having a chance to answer, he was saying, "Oh, I'm sorry. Can you let me know when you have a minute? I need something." That was the nicest thing he could have done for me. HE WAS OBSERVANT. He was a good manager.

Now the next time some cartoon character asks you this question, you can reply in two ways: the "right good solider way "or mine.

Question: Are you busy?

Answers:

1) No, I still have free time between midnight and 3:00 A.M.
2) Not yet, but when I start mopping the parking lot, look out.
3) No, I'm crazy. (You can add "for working here.")
4) Not yet, but I'm sure you'll fix that.
5) Sorry, the line forms to the left.
6) Take a number; they're outside.
7) I must be, you're here to mess with me.
8) Yes, doing all your work for you will do that.
9) Yes, this is called work. Do you recognize it?
10) No, I like pulling my hair out by the roots.
11) What was your clue, Sherlock?
12) Say, you must be sober today.
13) No, I like having to do the work of three people.
14) I'll tell you, but it'll cost you.
15) Just start laughing, and walk out until they leave.

And do you know what? Sometimes these Leaders will almost smile and even joke back when your wit outdoes them and shuts them up. (at first) Some people I work with will say, "Aren't you worried they will fire you"? I say "so". The reason people get walked on is because they won't fight back. Not me. I love it when I get a boss I can point out all the mistakes they make just as much as they point out mine. I am not trying to be a jerk, but if you dish it out, you should be able to take it. I try not to use profanity. That's what they do to you and expect back, so I just go the other way and outwit them. The knowledge that behind their forced smile is a seething madness, that wants to win this battle of wits but alas is unarmed is thrilling. Also the knowledge that this person can fire me at any point makes it all the more enticing. But 9 out of 10 times, they won't. (It's that 1 time you have to worry, and you can usually tell how far you can push it.) They need you, and if they don't, your job is in jeopardy anyway. They get rid of you. That's better bottom line, so what the hell.

All in all, I don't like being this way, but now you have to stand up for yourself. Most of these cretins need management training school to relearn that people are not just drones; they have families, and they have lives. But you know as well I do, FAT CHANCE. As I said, out of "what are you doing?" spawns a number of other less than profound questions. Another one is "are you working?" This is different from "are you busy?"

Definitions:

"Are you busy?" – They realize you are working but want you to drop everything you are doing because what they want is far more important then whatever you are doing because it is probably their work they want you to do. They just don't care about anyone else's orders; they just want it NOW!

"Are you working?" – They just think you live a life of leisure all day and do nothing but screw off and loaf and beat time.

I once unloaded two truckloads with six hundred items of freight drenched with sweat, dirty, hot, and tired. This poor excuse for a human came out of their air-condition office and asked me this. I guess he thought I took a hose, got myself wet, rolled around on the floor, and then a miracle occurred, the freight unloaded itself and put itself away.

4

Well, as you know, bosses think you are always trying to find ways to get out of work and steal their money. Now, there are a few which spoil it for everyone and do beat time on a regular basis. That makes it bad for everyone, but not everyone does it, and they should know this and have the smarts to know which one is which.

This is, however, reality, and they don't know who beats time and/or don't care. It is the one who does get out of work that is hunting buddy or fishing buddy or neighbor or whatever. So that leaves you and me to do the work and get yelled at for the one who does not. I worked with a person who had a boss that delegated all his work to someone else, and while the boss was outside smoking and saying how busy they were, this person was doing his work for him. Now that all good and well, but then this person got in trouble for not completing his own work from corporate and was told he should be more like his boss. (The boss took all the credit and then told corporate this person was a screw up.) That's a boss for ya. Push the work to someone else and take the credit for it. They show you how much pull they have and throw their weight around, and they get you in trouble for not doing what you were hired for. Amazing huh? I have seen it happen at 10 of my 22 jobs I have had, and it is always the same. We had a boss that hunted and fished with one of the employees (he had a 4x4), and this guy would get away with any thing he wanted. I seen this guy right in front of this boss beat time for 20 or 30 minutes while I was working and talking to this boss about the upcoming weekend hunting trip. Then this dolt asked me if I was working! Well I had a few answers for him, which he didn't like. (I had the nerve to speak up. You know, freedom of speech and all, they don't like that.) Well, needless to say, they told me I had a bad attitude. I had to laugh and walk away. This confused them, which was not hard to do anyway.

So the next time one of these feeble-minded fellows asks you, "are you working?"

You may reply with a nice "Yes ma'am" or "Yes sir"......Or my way.

Question: "Are you working?"

Answers:

1) Yes, but I'm not having any fun
2) Yes, but you can't be. You're out here asking me these damn fool questions.
3) No, I'm studying a mail order Management Training course, and the first lesson is to beat time…a lot
4) Don't you have something better to do, like ruin a company or something?
5) Yes, I'm trying to move this freight with my mind.
6) Gee, I don't know. You tell me, after all you always tell me. I'm not paid to think.
7) If you don't know, I'm not going to tell you.
8) Let me look at my employee handbook and get back with you.
9) I'm sorry… What's your name again?
10) Who woke you up?
11) Shhhh… It's naptime.
12) Well, what do you know? You can say a whole sentence.
13) Look out everyone, the genius is on the loose again.
14) It's hard to believe you get paid more than me.
15) Get the hell out of here, and let me do my job. Go find some poor unsuspecting animal to abuse.

I look at it like this. They want to be boneheads. Fine, let them. I can be just as bad if not worse. We all do our jobs to the best of our ability, and they know that, but they still want to show you who is boss. Well la-te-da. They don't need to throw their weight around. We know what we need to do. Why do they need to baby-sit us? I'll tell you why. They got to where they are (the bosses) by getting away with murder themselves, and now they are in a position of POWER, and they think everyone else is going to do the same. Ha! Not a chance! I never got anywhere but by good hard work and a sense of humor. The managers who I respect got to where they are the same way by hard work, putting up with the boss's tripe, and vowing never to do what was done to them. So why do we have bosses, you may ask? Good question. Why do we have hemorrhoids?

It's just a part of life and the wonderful world of the working class. To show you an example of a true hemorrhoid, I had this boss who called me into his office and said to me, "you are getting too dirty and don't you have any better clothes?" OK, fine. At the time I was a truck driver. (For those of who don't know, driving a truck is not the cleanest job.) Why would I want to wear designer clothes to start with? They also told me my hair was too long. I didn't wear ripped up clothes or anything, just work clothes. They were always clean when I started my day, not ripped up and no rude sayings on them. I do have couth. So I really didn't understand what he meant. As for as my hair, I am 6 foot 7 and 250 pounds. When my hair is short, I look like I am 9 feet tall and 98 pounds. So I keep it a little long. My hair was always clean and kept under a hat and in a ponytail. For three years they didn't even know how long my hair was. That's how smart these people are. So I asked this brainchild, "Well, sir, I help unload, and in a lot of situations I unload it myself with no help. What do you expect?" He said the company was going to buy me uniforms that would keep me cleaner. I didn't understand that line of thinking, but I didn't question and said OK. The next day they handed me a company credit card and said go find them. Now I am six foot seven and two hundred and thirty five pounds; I don't find clothes just anywhere. So I looked and looked at all the discount stores; nothing in my size. Then I got a thought; I have the Company Credit CARD! SO I went to the highest priced place I could and found the right color pants and shirts. The pants were $78.95 apiece and the shirts were $55.95 apiece. Now they told me I could purchase three sets (Even though I asked aren't there five days in a week? I was told that was all I needed.) So I had the salesperson call my boss and tell him the price. Well, I could tell by the look on this poor man's face the answer was no. He then handed the phone to me and asked me could I find what I needed somewhere cheaper. I told him if you could find uniform pants in my size of 34 waist and 37 length, you do it. That was the end of the uniforms.

If all he wanted me to do was just wear uniforms, that was fine. But to come up with a lie like that and then tell me well these will keep you cleaner, I mean come on. I may have been born at night, but it wasn't last night. If I would have gotten uniforms, I would have had dirty uniforms at the end of the day, and if I didn't, I wouldn't have done my job right. So that is just another story of how the bosses are a big pain in the (well, you know, the hemorrhoid area).

We all have these bosses that think they, and only they, know best what is the right way to do things. And when you call them on something, you're considered a troublemaker or a smart-ass. Not that you're defending yourself; it is just that you have an attitude. Well maybe I do, but these nit-wits gave it to me to start with, and as another old saying goes, you reap what you sow. They come up with this stupid stuff. I just point out the errors in their logic and try to keep cool. That's what the most important thing is; you have to stay calm and make it into a joke, or you will lose the battle of wits. They don't know how to handle someone who is calm in the face of their anger, or when they try to mess with you or try some dumb-ass question. Stay cool and use the quick wit and straight face tactic; it works everytime. It confuses them (which at times isn't hard to do). They think just because they are yelling, you should be also, or if they ask you some strange question, you should just understand or quake in your boots or something. I made the mistake of yelling back once, and they turned it around on me and said, "Is that how you talk to customers?" When I realized what I had done, I went back to being calm and said, "No, I respect them." This ended the whole thing right there, and that's is the way it should be. Don't go down to their level and act like them. Just stay calm, and as I said, use your mind because they don't. It is a battle of the mind between you and a boss so you are already a step ahead of them. And sometimes you have to stand up for yourself; you have to put your two cents to these useless pieces of air space, unless you like being a doormat and believe me, your boss had big shoes with a lot of B.S. on the bottom. So the "Is that how you talk to customers" is the next issue we will be looking into and why they would say such things.

"Is that how you talk to customers?"

This is when you have them on the run and they are outwitted. (And they know it!) This question is one of the last resorts they can use. (As I said, one of the last but not the only.) I know this person who had this boss come out, just scream at this poor worker, and run off so many obscenities that it made me blush. The bad part is that this poor unsuspecting soul had no idea what this melon-head was screaming about!

He just went on and on about how bad it was and so forth and so on. At last, the poor person broke and screamed back, and then this question came up, "Is that how you talk to customers?" Now correct me if I'm wrong, but wasn't the boss the one who came out to form this meeting of the minds? (with his absent) And I'm sorry, but I would get mad at this also, especially if I didn't do whatever the hell he was screaming about. And when the boss said that all that they could do was look away embarrassed and walk away (with the boss smiling to himself or herself). This just burned me so I found ways to give it back to them, and now I look forward to confrontations like this just so I can make them feel like us for a change. In my opinion, this person showed great patience holding out that long. I, as would anyone, would not and could not do it. I also would have gotten mad, but now anymore I just smile and write it down. I mean, what the hell, I can find another job and have found other jobs. So the next time you find yourself in this position you can let the boss yell, or yell back at them. Or you can use my answers, or at least come up with your own answers to solve this. Remember, don't get mad if you can help it. That is what they want. That means they win, and that is not the way it should be in these kinds of games.

Question: "Is that how you talk to customers?"

Even more witty answers (OK smart-assed answers)

Answers:

1) No, I respect them.
2) No, but you ought to hear what they say about you.
3) No, they aren't as stupid as you are.
4) No, they understand plain English.
5) No, they have a mind that is able to do two things at once.

6) Well, now, let me think about that one……(then just walk away)
7) Is this a trick question?
8) I don't talk to them; it is not in my job description.
9) I don't have too. They know how bad you are. They don't need me telling them why I yell.
10) Yes, it's how I get my jollies.
11) No, my name is not (insert boss's name here).
12) If I did, don't you think you would have fired me by now considering how nice and understanding a boss you are?
13) No, I like them.
14) No, but maybe I should start. Look where you are, and if you can do it, so can I. Thank you for your inspiration.
15) No, why should I? I am trying to change the company image. I am trying to be nice to them.

"Let me show you the right way to do that"

Oh, my, where I could go with this (and I will). I had a boss once. Everything this book is written about and more than I could fit in two more books is written just for this joker. He was the epitome of all time bosses, the king of them all. I will go into more detail of his misgivings later, but for now I will start with this. No matter what you were doing, he would always know a better way how to do it and how long it should take. He would always say, "LET ME SHOW YOU THE RIGHT WAY." And even though it would always blowup in his face, he would try anyway to show you his way of doing it. So we let him (and laughed at him later). One example of this dunderhead is the time he cut off his own finger. Yes, I said cut off his finger. He was showing a new person how not to use a cutting machine. Now in order to do this feat of mental genius, you would have to try to climb up the side of the machine and put your hand where it should never go in order to show someone what could happen. He had a piece of paper to cut so he could show this new person how this cutter worked, and when he did, he missed with the paper and cut off his own finger. Now after we found it and got him

to a hospital, he was alright and all went back to normal (except for
the echoes of laughter) Pretty good showing someone how not to get
hurt by getting hurt. This way of doing things would not have
occurred to me. And the bad part of all this is this kind of person is
not limited. They come in all shapes and sizes, ages and sexes. You
never know where or when you might run across one until you are
under them as an employee. Then it is too late. But that is where my
book comes in handy. You will be able to tell where these people are,
or if you are already there, how to handle them with finesse, or at
least laugh at them. Either way you win. And, as I said, the bad part
is these brain dead people are all over no matter where you go, always
wanting to show you the right way to do something. (I guess they
nerve heard of undefended thought.) I will get into more of this type
of person later in the book. As you will see they span all sorts of ways
of being a boss.

"Handbooks"

This is what I call an adult comic book. Why do they kill trees
for this waste of time and paper? It all depends on who you are with a
boss as to how the handbook affects you. As I have stated earlier,
bosses, not true managers, do this type of treatment. They should have
more and better things to do with paper than this. I could name at least
one……
(And it is what I do with it too, flush it). They hand you the
"company handbook" and expect you to remember every detail by the
next day because they sure will and sometimes will have a whole new
meaning than what's stated in it. But it will be you who won't
understand what is in it. Even if you are a lawyer, you would not get
the meaning of "the company handbook."

To give one example of this, in mine it said, "an employee can
be terminated for…," then it gave some reasons, and at the end it
continued. Here's the kicker: "OTHER REASONS." Now excuse
me, but what would the other reasons be? One person was fired
because they didn't load a truck right. The company said it looked
sloppy. Now this person was new, and they left them by themselves.

They did the best they could but was let go anyway. Like I said, other reasons can mean a vast number of things depending on who you are. (And what part of WHO's anatomy you can kiss) There were other people who did such things, like run a forklift off the dock and into someone's van but was not fired. Go figure.

Another good example of a boss's wonderful way of thinking is this one: "Any confrontations of any kind will not be tolerated. It is grounds for termination." Now correct me if I'm wrong, but isn't it true that if a boss yells at you, that is a confrontation? Or, when you ask in a nice way, say maybe why your check is short 10 hours, that is a confrontation? Or, if you ask nicely why did they change your hours without telling you with a little notice a confrontation? Well maybe not at all places, but at some of the ones I have had the displeasure to work at, it was. I once asked why my check was 15 hours short and was told, didn't I read the handbook? I should have put it in a written request as to why my check was short, then they would have looked into it and let me know. Even when I had a copy of my time card in my hand to show them, they didn't want to hear it. It is just another good example of how these pea brains think, and I am not the only one that goes through this. I have talked to a lot of people to do this book, not just myself, and the same holds true to everyone I have talked to. A boss is melon head, and the higher you go, the bigger the melon. As you might have guessed, I have ways to avoid this also and ways to piss them off in the process. First some more examples of a handbook. You will call in sick to work one half-hour before you start and will call back one half before your shift is over to let the company know if you will be in the next day.

OK, that may sound like a good idea, but if you were like my friend, he opened the place up and was the only one there for an hour. Even though it was a big company and had lots of employees, they only had him come in to open. Who should they call? My friend often wondered what would happen if he were sick. They fired my friend one time because he had to go to the hospital and didn't call in. Needless to say, though he did get his job back after my friend got a lawyer. Then they had two people open from that point on. Do not wear clothes that show off body parts. Now I have a tale that will make you laugh. We had a fellow that worked for us. He always wore a half shirt and shorts in the warehouse. Now the boss saw him one day and just got up on the wrong side of bed and just wanted to mess with someone. Well he picked this fellow. He had been wearing the same type of clothes since he started 13 years prior to this event, so as to why the boss thought he could rattle his cage is beyond me. The boss walked up to him and yelled, "DON'T YOU READ THE HANDBOOK? I want you to dress better tomorrow." The employee just smiled and said, "OK, I will". So the next day came, and here he comes with a tighter pair of shorts and a shorter half shirt. He said to the foreman, "Let me know when the boss gets here." So when the boss's car pulled into the parking lot, we all told him, "here he comes." So this fellow brought a tie with him and put it on. Well the boss wanted to check to see if this employee did what he asked and came out to look. He saw him from the back and started yelling. When he turned around, the employee had the tie on and smiled and said, "Hi boss". No more was said. The boss just went back into the office and never bothered this fellow again. Like I said, handbooks are like adult comic books; they are entertaining but really useless when push comes to shove. We didn't have one for 15 years at one place of employment. The rules were always up in the air so they could change them at will.

I know this sounds like a lot of hooey, but it is true. One time there would be one thing we couldn't do and then the next week it would be ok, but that depends on who was doing it also. Another rule I have seen in a handbook was this: "DON'T USE YOUR COMPUTER FOR VIEWING PORNO PICTURES." Yes, I am not kidding. It had this in there. What should be common sense is now on print. I mean how many of us do this real dumb move? I'm not saying that no one has ever done this, but as I said, some things should be common sense and not need to be written down. If you have time to look at dirty pictures on your computer then you have too much free time on your hands.

Here is another one: "DO NOT TAKE COMPANY EQUIPMENT HOME TO USE OR SELL." Ok, once again, we have something that should have never been printed on paper. But corporate thinks they have to lead you by the hand for something that should have again been common sense and that should have sunk in on the first day you were there. Easy, NO STEALING. But nope. They have to make a big long hairy issue out it. Oh, well, if they didn't, I would not have anything to write about. Let's get into some other things that "handbooks" have in them.

Here is another one: "DO NOT TAKE LONGER THAN YOUR ALLOTTED TIME ON BREAKS OR LUNCH." This is another one that should have never been written. The person who wrote this should have been choked by his own typewriter ribbon. With this in there they can say such witty statements as, "Didn't you read the handbook?" when a simple verbal statement should have been enough. Every little detail is in writing. It reads like stereo instructions on these handbooks. By the time you learn it, you are already violating it. And they don't give you the time (as if there would be enough in a month to learn it) to find out what you are expected to know. SO then they hang it over your head as if you are a great sinner, and if you don't act like a servant to them, they can drop the proverbial shoe on you. They don't forget even if it was your first week. Oh, well, as I said, there are ways to deal with that also. "STARTING TIME FOR DRIVERS ARE BETWEEN 7:00 AND 10:00." This is another brain dead rule that the company put in. They told one driver that it allows more flexibility for the company to adjust your starting time. But I as you might have guessed, I found a way around it. This is a easy one to work around so to speak. I come at 7:00 or at 7:10 or at 7:15, and when they try to yell at me for being late, I just inform them that according to the contract, page two, halfway down, it says, and I quote the line for them. I also tell them that I wanted them to take that out at one time, but they insisted on keeping it in. So I use it to my advantage. As I have said, rules are made to be bent in the handbook, or at least some of them, the others are so obvious that they should have never been in there. Now that we know that…

Question: "Didn't you read the handbook on that?"

Some more of the answers that would be considered witty

Answers:

1) Handbook? I thought it was a novel.
2) Yes, I did, your highness.
3) No, I have not gotten it back from my lawyer yet (because only he could understand most of it).
4) Yes, but as many times as you change the rules, I didn't think it mattered.
5) No, I have a life.
6) No, I need a week off to do it.
7) No, I think my puppy is though.
8) No, right now it is under one chair leg. At my rate of pay, I can't buy a new chair.
9) Yes, but I found it boring and with no real plot.
10) Yes, they should make a movie out of it like "How to make your employees suffer."
11) Yes, I did. Why? Was I supposed to take it seriously?
12) Yes, someone writes great fiction.
13) Am I getting paid to do that?
14) No, I plan to do it when nothing is better on TV, and I need a good laugh.
15) No, I had my child take it to school to show all the children as to why they need a good education and not to work for someone like you.

(No 15 is the one I like the most, but any will have the same reaction)

Peter Shelton

Chapter 2

Who do you think you are?

This is still another example of corporate intelligence, or as I say, boss's mentality. They are now mad and want to "get into it with you." Well, all I have to say is fat chance! A cooler head prevails and wins every time. For example, as I said, I was a truck driver once, and one day I was on a run. Well, three people refused some freight and my next stop was in front of the freight that was refused. SO I called in and told the dispatcher what was up. They said come on in. So I came in, and the president of the company was waiting for me. He started yelling and cussing at me and asked me who do I think I was. Well even before I could answer, he yelled that he would dock my overtime, and I would pay for the delivery for a cab to take that freight out to the customer with my overtime pay, even though I could not get to the customer's freight. Well then he started yelling even more and told me to unload that truck. Well, I said, since I was not getting paid to do it now, I am going home; unload it yourself. I mean, I tried to explain to this thistlehead, but he would not listen to reason, so I left. I did not yell. I did not cuss back. All I did was leave. The next day he called me into his office and asked me that question again: who do you think you are? This time I answered him, and I was never bothered again. Yes, I still had a job there.

They ask this question when they have little or no way to beat you verbally. It just occurs to them that "Hey I am a boss, and I rule you." Wrong. They may be a boss but rule, No. They ask this when they are so mad that they can't think (which is most of the time). They think if they try to scare you that you will give in and kiss their feet because you have a job there and think you will never leave. Again WRONG. You and I were looking when we came across this one and can do it again. When people realize that they need us more than we need them, things will change a lot faster, but until then, you have people like me to poke fun at them all.

Peter Shelton

Question: Who do you think you are?

Some answers that will arise their anger:

Answers:

1) I think I am a person who made a mistake. I took a job here.
2) You pay me, don't you know?
3) I am not paid to think. Remember, you told me that.
4) If I have to think it will cost you overtime.
5) Wow, did you think of that all by yourself?
6) I am the one that you abuse, remember?
7) I am the one that you love to hate.
8) I am a disgruntled employee.
9) I am the company scapegoat, sir.
10) I am the company whipping post.
11) An underpaid, overworked employee.
12) If you don't know by now, I am not going to tell you.
13) You don't know? And to think, you're my supervisor.
14) I think I am one of your employees who needs to redo my resume.
15) You're a fine one to ask me about thinking since you do so little of it yourself.

"Oh you're a smart ass"

By now I am sure that you know I might have seen this one come up on occasion. Yes I have, and more than once, as you might have guessed. I am not really as bad as I sound. Ok, maybe I am, but they started this game so I just play too. I mean if they didn't want smart-assed answers, they should not have asked me a stupid question to start with, and we would have gotten along just fine. But as you see from this book, and I know that you have been in the same kinds of situations as me, we both know better.

You see when you answer back to a boss or corporate they think you are a troublemaker and not just a free thinking person, and it scares them because they don't understand that concept. "What? Someone has a free thought here? Dock them for 2 hours." That is their mindset. They think that if you have an independent thought you may do something they won't like (like find another job, let's say) and that is not good for the other workers to see. You just may have a mutiny. So they frown on independent thinking. They don't want you to think. If they did, they wouldn't say such things. But bosses will never learn, but the rest of us do. That's why we have such things as songs about bad bosses and jobs and written rhyme about bosses and yes, you guessed it, books about bosses. You would think by now that maybe, just maybe, that they would have gotten the hint. They always lose in such things, and I don't know a lot of people who like their bosses. I have known people to like their managers but never a boss as described in this book. They come in all races and genders and such but share one thing in common; they all lack brains and/or common sense. A boss lacks what we use everyday. If we acted like they do, we would lose our job. Can you imagine what would happen if we thought like some of them? All the work would be delegated to someone else and nothing would get done but paperwork, and most of it would be wrong. and we would have to hire someone to fix it. So with that in mind, we go on to the infamous question.

Question: Oh, you're a smart-ass?

Here are some more answers that will raise an eyebrow.

1) No, I am a dumb-ass. I still work here.
2) Smart-ass hell! Working here isn't that smart.
3) Oh my, with such witty statements like that, I just don't know how to reply
4) You're the reason cousins should never marry.
5) Well at least in my case I have one part of my body that has intelligence, which is one more than you.
6) Just trying to keep it from being boring sir.
7) No, that's in my job description.
8) Will I get a raise if I say yes?

9) I am so sorry, sir (or ma'am), I beg your forgiveness you holiness.
10) No, I was and am not trying for your position; my knees couldn't take it.
11) No, but I am willing to learn.
12) Well, now that's a question.
13) Nope. I am a lazy ass. The smart-ass left early.
14) Don't you have something better to do other than giving your people grief, like haunt a house?
15) GET BENT! (Only use if all else fails)

The first was just the beginning of what is all throughout this book. It was an introduction. Now we start to get into the meat of things. As I said earlier, bosses are a funny sort of people (even though no one laughs). Their whole thing in life is to make themselves look good while doing and/or buying as little as possible, to delegate the work off to some one else, or to make someone use a piece of equipment that should have been in the dumpster years ago, or even to keep the shelves bare of stock to make the bottom line look better (even if it means that no one can buy anything because it is out of stock, their idea of thinking is that if they come in, maybe they will buy something else). Don't ask me. I have yet to figure that one out either, but it happens again and again, and I just shake my head. (But yet I am the smart-ass who doesn't know anything) As this next chapter unfolds, we will look at many aspects of a boss's head. I know. I bet some of you are saying, "that shouldn't take very long," but believe it or not, a boss's mind is very complex. (Not that it helps having more than one personality inside you) A boss, unlike any other form of life, can change from a sheep to a viper in a matter of milliseconds and then right back again. It is an amazing sight to behold, indeed to witness, this phenomenon unfold.

You first have in front of you this calm, alluring person pleasant to be around and fun to talk to. Then the demon comes out, the face changes to a reddest purple, and the voice growls becoming almost more than a human ear can bear without flinching, and the growls and barks of this inept beast become profane and without sense of what they are doing. Then they revert back to the docile state all within the matter of minutes and don't even remember who they talked to or what they did or said. A sudden case of amnesia occurs. So I have found studying the boss that this complex individual has many sides to their personality. (Of course we always get the backside) Some bosses have more sides than others, just like their backsides are wider than others. Some have one or two, and others have many to boggle your mind. Then some have just one, but 9 out of 10 times the one is not what you really need or want. I don't have enough paper or time to discuss the realms of their actions or their many personalities, but we will hit on the ones we all see everyday even when they are not our bosses, and we see what they are doing to everyone else, the ones that do the most changing from the one person to the next, and then back, the ones who ask such questions like we will discuss as who do you think you are? (Thought I forgot didn't you? I'll get to it.) The ones who always ask questions but never really want an answer, "Just see things my way or else," those kinds of bosses, the ones we all love to hate and/or just shake our heads and ask ourselves, How did they get to the position that they are in? (We all know how, but I am trying to keep it a clean book.)

So let's just jump in headlong and talk about the first question, shall we? Who do you think you are? There are different variations of this. "Who in the hell do you think you are?" "Do you think you're funny?" "Do you think this attitude will help?" and so forth and so on. It all boils down to the same thing: thinking. (Which is something bosses seldom do) They ask you a question like this, but really don't want a answer. They want you to cower in a corner and be a good little worker and not speak your mind or voice your opinion, which I might add is still your right to do so as long as you don't show disrespect toward your employer (at least not too much). Let's face it, you're there to work, not to be anyone's whipping post, and some bosses get carried away (and some should be carried away). If you let yourself become a doormat, you can bet the some boss will wipe their feet on your back. I say, stand up, speak up. The worst they can do is fire you, and as they say, you were looking when you found this one, and they probably would've done it anyway no matter what you may have or not have said. So you might as well have fun in the process. So when these drooling nitwits ask you a question like "Who do you

21

think you are?" that means in boss terms that you are outsmarting me, and I don't like it. They have their own language; it is based upon themselves.

Example 1:   "Why are you doing it like that?" This means you're not doing it my way.

Example 2:   "What did you do to it?" means that I need to blame someone else for it being broken and take attention away from the fact that it has been ready to break for a while, and I didn't want to fix it.

Example 3:   "You need to have a better attitude." This means that you have to learn that we are not going to change a thing, and even though we all know what's wrong, we don't want to talk about it.

Example 4:   "We need to look into the ramifications of this." This means simply, yeah right, in your dreams.

Example 5:   "We need to reduce the cost of operations and trim out some things that are luxuries." This means we need to fire some people to get a better bottom line and a bigger bonus at the end of the year.

Example 6:   "We care about our employees' heath insurance. That's why we are now changing to this company to give them the best we think we can." This means they found a cheaper rate.

Example 7:   "What do you need from us to make your job easier?" This means if it is easy then they can fire you for not doing twice as much.

Example 8:   "We can't give any raises this year. We had a bad year, and we all must pull in our belt a little." This means I need a new car, and the belt they are referring to on them is their money belt, and the reason they are pulling it in is because they are hiding it.

Example 9:   "We know that you have a family also and would like to have time with them." This can mean two things. The first meaning is "but we don't care." The second is "so that's why we are letting you go so you can spend more time with them."

Example 10:   "You're getting paid so what's your beef?" This
                      means they can afford beef, you can't, and they don't
                      plan to do anything about it anyway.

        The list could go on and on, but these are the ten I will use in
this chapter the most.
        The reason bosses have their own language is because of how
complex their mind is and the way it works. Notice I did not say if it
was an efficient way, just complex. Complex can mean a whole lot of
different things; it can mean that they are an independent thinker and
tie things together, or it can mean that they can work on six different
things at once, or that their way of thinking is so advanced that most
won't understand it, or the boss's way that you don't have the
slightest clue on where the hell he got that idea or what the hell he is
talking about and neither do they. (It just sounds good and looks
goods on paper.) In the case of this book the latter is the complex
which we shall speak of here.
        And for those of you wondering, I am adding everyday to this
book. You could call this a labor of love or something. In other
words, not only do I know of wherefore I speak, but I live it everyday.
Trust me, it has gotten interesting and sad that bosses have sunk so
low nowadays. Here is one that happened 2 years after I started this
book. It happened, as a matter of fact, today. Remember the
language I spoke of? Well this is a good example. I went job hunting
because my company was selling out, and I went to a big corporation,
a service place. I won't mention any names, as I have said. Anyway,
the place was a pig's sty for starters, and they handed me a
application. So I went into the next room and started it. When I got
to the last page, it was a questionnaire which consisted of, and I
quote, "How many felonies have you been convicted of in the last 36
months?" All, yes not just one, but all the questions were like this. It
wasn't have you ever been convicted of but how many have you done.
Now I didn't mind too much after I needed a job, but what bothered
me most was the second page of that questioner quote: please describe
yourself to us we will only hire nice and helpful people." Ok, I can
even handle that, but when I was filling it out there were two or three
people behind me cussing out customers after they had hung up and

using the "f" word loud enough to hear them outside, and there were ladies in the room with us, and they were talking about spitting on the others guy's truck and so forth and so on.

That got me real mad so I tore up the paperwork and left and called, at my own expense, the head office and informed them. I told them that for a service based company that's not the kind of image that they want to project, and if they paid more, they just might get real people, not just some yahoos that want an easy job. I was told that "our people are paid more than enough, and I should keep my opinions to myself." So I told them, "What kind of recommendation do you think I would give anyone who might want to use your service after I saw what I was exposed to sir?" Then I told them for a serviced-based company that is not the way to make friends and influence people and to keep ahead of the competition. I was told that I didn't know what the hell I was talking about and got hung up on.

Like I said, their own language, that means the company doesn't give a damn about the place. All they want is bottom line. Here we go again, that phrase again, I know, I know, but tell me I am wrong here. If you're in a business to service customers, shouldn't you be concerned customers? Just my two cents, I guess, which is more than most bosses in corporate should be paid. Ahh, the language of bosses, it is one of a kind that we should all hire an interpreter to figure it out, and you might think I am just kidding here, but how many times have you heard this? Let's say, for instance, you're on a 10 minute break. You just got there, and you lit up a smoke (or not if you don't), or you're just enjoying your break. Then out of nowhere a boss comes out and says, "come on, these twenty minute breaks are killing our company," or something like that kind of statement. Well now in "boss's language" that means I can't stand to see anyone not doing anything because I am paying for it even though you earned it.

It says in your good OLE handbook that you are allowed two ten or fifteen minute breaks, but your boss thinks otherwise.

They think that you are beating time, or they think that you are trying to get their money so their watch is always fast, and no matter if they saw you go out on break, hell even if they went with you, they think you take too long for break. And yes, that leads me into another wise question that they ask, "Are you beating time?"

Uh-huh, I know it is another one of those that a lot of people have never heard but a lot of us have. These questions all have a few things in common.

1) They are all stupid.
2) They are all asked by the person that should not even be allowed to play with the remote control.
3) They are all questions some of us have heard and some of the questions all of us have heard at one time or another.

So no one is left out here. Every one of us has answered one or more of these questions at one point in our life or another. Some of us, unfortunately, have had to answer more than one or two. Nonetheless, we all know that these brain-fried questions have come up so we shall attempt to answer them.

"Are you beating time?"

The first time I heard this one come up was at a place I worked at for a short time, and it wasn't me it was asked to. Nope, that's right, I got out of it somehow. Anyway, this dolt of a boss was watching us work one day, and a co-worker and I were working with lumber. We were cutting it up and throwing the bad and warped pieces away, about 200 boards worth of bad lumber. So we went to take a break. I went into the bathroom, and this other poor fellow got caught. When I was finished in the bathroom, I came out, and this boss was yelling at this guy and throwing out a slew of profanities saying that he was beating time. Now, mind you, we had worked through our lunch to get this done for him, but that wasn't enough. He wanted more. About the time the question came up about beating time, he saw me and stopped and said that this fellow had slowed me down also. I then proceeded to tell him the error of his ways. Nothing was said to us the rest of the day. When this question pops up, there are two rules with it before you answer it.

1) Never lose you temper, and with this question it can happen really easily.
2) Always smile when you answer it.

Question: "Are you beating time?"

Here are some answers that you might like to use.

1) Yes, I learned from the best, you sir.
2) No, sir, I done whipped it.
3) If you don't like this speed, you're going to hate the next one I have.
4) Gotta have time to spare to beat first sir.
5) Yes, this sweat is all from not doing anything.
6) Time who?
7) Now I am. Can't answer these questions and work at the same time.
8) Who me? Never would I do such a thing...... Sir.
9) I though beating was your department.
10) I wish I could but someone has to work around here you sure don't.
11) Beat time? Why thank you, I need a break. (Then just walk away)
12) 12) Wasn't that in the handbook? I had better look it up.
13) No, but I did hit the time clock if that classifies.
14) How could anyone beat time around here with such observant people like you watching us by the way your fly is down.
15) No, I am looking into the ramifications of resting for 10 minutes.

You may think that "Are you beating time" and "Are you working" are one in the same but not in the eyes of a boss. As I have been saying, they have their own language and those two statements, hell even the same statement, can have many different meanings. All depends on the situation so I must cover as many as I know and then some so I can translate the best that I can, but even I will have missed some. (Thus the lead in for my next book)

You didn't follow procedure.

All I want to know is who's Procedure? This rule makes no sense to me because it can change on a daily basis and depending on which boss it was that told you what procedure they wanted you to use. For example, we needed a part for a machine to make it work so I told one supervisor about it, the part number, what it did, and why we needed it. Now that was the boss that I was always told that I should have gone to for these kinds of things. Now a month goes by and the part was still not there, so I asked the boss where it was or have they heard anything. About that time a boss that was over this one piped up and said, "No we don't need that. I called in a welder to fix that. He should be here in a few days." Now call me stupid, but a welder would have cost more money than if we would have just ordered a new part. So again I tried to explain to this other poor excuse for a human being that the machine doesn't work without the part and that I had ordered that part through this other boss. I showed him my report as to why we needed it and to explain that the new part would have cost less than a welder. He yelled that I should have followed procedure and talked to him first, and he would have straightened me out on just who's boss around here.

Ok at first I didn't say anything, then the welder showed up, and it was a friend of this "Boss man" who said I didn't follow procedure. Well, this welder should not have been allowed to play with matches let alone weld anything. He started two small fires and ruined the connecting part that was very expensive and the machine was really toast then. So I then went into the Big Boss's office and told him to come take a look at the nice fires we had, the damage it had done, how well he did his welding (considering the attaching part was now a molten mass of metal), that his uncle Harry, or whoever, also got burned while he was welding, and wanted to know if the company was going to pay for his doctor bill for this little endeavor. Well that statement went over like a lead balloon, and I was told that I had a bad attitude. Ok, I can deal with that, but I now was sent out to get the parts myself and now not just one but two parts. The one we needed to begin with was $15; the other part (the one that the welder turned into a blob of smoldering metal) was about $200. Plus the welder's bill was $700 between his services rendered and his doctor's bill.

So I just sat back and had a good laugh about it all. It would have been fixed in ten minutes, but since we had another piece to put on, it took two days to do it. Here is another good example of not following procedure. I had a guy who was a danger to work around at any given time. We were working on truck that had to be unloaded by hand and were taking the stock to the shelves, putting it in the area it needed to be. He got into a hurry and started throwing this stuff harder and harder. It weighed about 100 pounds for one item, and guess who was hit with it? Yep, that's right, me. He had pinned my wrist between a steel bar and this item really well. I told the supervisor about it, showed him the bruise and the swollen wrist, and asked to go to the doctor. Well, he said no in front of another person, so I didn't do anything about it at first, just hoped it would be ok. About two days later it hurt so badly that I went to the hospital and had them check it. I had cracked my wrist bone. I got back to the job, and my boss just blew sky high. He told me I didn't follow procedure, and he was going to fire me. That was until I had told him that I tried to tell the supervisor and asked him to go to the doctor and was told no. He didn't believe me at first. I said well wait a second. I brought in the fellow who had seen this, and he confirmed it. So I was no longer in trouble, but the supervisor was. Once again the boss put his mouth where his brain should have been. Before he blew up and threatened to fire me, he should have found out what the situation was and why I had gone on my own to the doctor.

The following morning they wanted me to sign a paper stating that I was not refused to go to the doctor (of course I didn't) and told me, and I quote, "I thought you were kidding me about that." My reply was, "Yeah, my wrist turns blue and swells up all the time." So for a month no one would talk to me, which didn't hurt my feelings a bit. And the funny part about all of this is the bosses don't even know or care what they had done. I could have sued them big time for not sending me to the doctor, but I never did. I just always reminded them of the fact that I could have. (That was more fun.) So when a boss says, "You didn't follow procedure," this leads me into a kind of boss that is dreaded by all…THE BUS DRIVER! A primate among bosses, this kind is everywhere. There is no getting away from these cretins. A Bus Driver is the kind of boss, and I have seen this with my own eyes, that says there is only one Bus Driver here and I am it! A prime example of "The Bus Driver" is you are working on a program, let's say, and it is a main frame program. Main frame computers control all other computers that are linked to it. So anyway it will take you about five minutes to fix a problem in the main frame. So instead of shutting down the main frame, which can take up to 30 minutes to start back up, for five minutes of work, you just go in to the program and take control for five minutes and fix it and you're back on. Quick and easy, on and right back off, but oh man are you in trouble. You didn't follow procedure! Most of the time you should so don't get me wrong here, but sometimes you shouldn't waste the time for something simple.

Even if you do follow procedure, you shouldn't have to follow it to the letter each and every time because situations come up, and it is a do or die kind of thing for some things. Either you fix it before it gets real bad, or you wait and go through the motions and hope and pray that it will wait for you. Even if you do follow procedure to the letter every time, "The Bus Driver" changes the rules from person to person, or day to day, depending on what mood they are in. This is a great game of chance, a roll of the dice if you will. But before you spin that roulette wheel, please check three things:

1) The day of the week. This has a lot to do with it. If it is a Monday, don't try this without a net. Mondays are bad because the bosses are in a poor sense of inner self (probably from being hung over).

2) Who is going to be most affected by what you may or may not do? This falls under if I do this my boss may be the one most affected by it. Well that may be good or bad, depending on what it is. Like for instance, if the computer system will format itself, you don't wait and go in and fix it, then I would say go with it mainly because it will save you the headache of trying to fix it later. But if the boss is online, and you want to fix it, may be a slight problem if they are playing bingo or something.

3) Last, but not least, check the lunar cycle. You never know when your boss will change their mind, and that's a good enough excuse for them as any.

You may ask why should I try if I get into trouble? Well for those who say it can't be done, get out of the way for those who are doing it. Sometimes a bit of incentive will get you a long way in life, unless you have a Bus Driver for a boss. Then you will get lecture number 108 on the proper procedure on whatever the hell it was you didn't do right which lasts about 2 1/2 hours. When you have to endure your next "You didn't follow procedure" ear-bending, these are some amusing anecdotes you can reply with.

Question: You didn't follow procedure.

Some more sayings to give to your bus driver.

1) Sure I did......What day is it, and I'll tell you which one I had written down from the last time we had this chat?
2) It is hard to follow a procedure coming from someone who can't fold a road map.
3) Which one? You change procedures as many times as I change my socks.
4) Which yellow brick road do you want me to go down this time?
5) I bet you have a procedure to use the bathroom.
6) I tried, but I lost my novel you call a handbook.
7) No, I didn't. I wanted it done before I retired.
8) Yes I did......Oh sorry that was last month's procedure.
9) No, I didn't remember my mother's maiden name to fill out the forms.
10) That's what I get for thinking again.
11) No, I didn't know that I had to tell you that I was independently thinking.
12) I didn't? Hmmmmmmmm (then just walk away)
13) No, I did it my way and fixed it right the first time.
14) No, I didn't; my mother always told me not to talk to dolts.
15) Yes, I did. I even did it with a smile.

Moving right along, the next thing that comes up is independent thought. How many times have you heard that you should free-think that we want people that can think on the fly, or we want people that make decisions? As I have said before, bosses have their own language, and what it really means is that we want people that understand that we are the ones that make the important decisions and don't forget it. That is what bosses mean by wanting people that can think. They want to make sure you know who is the big cheese, the head honcho, the bus driver. And what also falls under that bill is being in charge. No one is really in charge of anyone unless you are a boss or owner. That is a fake title and an unjust insult to any one who can think. Bosses are funny that way. They lure you into the fold just like a lamb to the wolf and move in for the big kill. I was "in charge" of six people once, and I had my own way of doing things. I always got things done faster than any other group in the plant, but it wasn't done by procedure or by asking for independent thought from any boss. (I didn't think I needed to ask for permission to think.) Well, one day as luck would have it, a boss came by to see me; they wanted to know how I did it so they could look into doing it in other areas. After I told them and showed them the how's and the why's, he admitted that is was a great way of getting things done, but I needed to quit doing it that way. I asked why. I have upped production and gotten more done than any other one here. I was told that's not the way we do things. The main gripe was that when I unloaded a truck or anyone else did, instead of putting all the freight in the front then checking it off, I put it into stock and checked it off. Then I looked for orders and filled them A.S.A.P. and got them out the door so I had room for the next truck. Or sometimes we had a truck to load in the next door so I took off of one truck and then put it on the other truck if we had orders for it, rather than put it into stock and then pull it back out later that day. Nope, don't do it anymore. We need to keep this as it has been for the last 20 years and do it the old way even if it means that production goes down and time is wasted. "I (the boss) did this same job for 30 years like this, and it works better. Too much chance for mistakes your way." My reply was, "well I can read sir, and I would have to pull it anyway and check it off anyway." Went in one ear and out the other (because nothing was there to stop it). A month later my way of doing things was this boss's idea, and he switched all the groups to do it like I had been doing it for three years. He said it was a corporate idea. Independent thought worked well as long as it is a boss's, and not yours. What makes you mad about it is that corporate hasn't had a clue all this time that the workers (like us) who really drive the bus and not the people in charge like the bosses (who most of the time just get in the way). It is not a crime to think for yourself. Most managers (note I said MANAGERS) like people to think on their own and have a certain assertiveness about themselves. Bosses, on the other hand, don't want anyone to get ahead of them by hard work and doing the right thing. It may make them look bad, which wouldn't take a brain surgeon to make a boss look bad.

A boss wants to keep his thumb on an employee and make sure they know who is the main person in charge. "The Bus Driver," this term will come out a lot from this point on. In this chapter I will explain all about this term and meaning, but for now you'll have to trust me on this. One independent thought and action may turn out bad or good, depends on how well something worked, but a manager will praise someone for trying, a boss will not. They will either take the idea and/or credit for something and tell you that it should have been done like that a month ago. You see, the boss is an insecure person, always worried about their place in the scheme of things, and never wanting to lose whatever place they now have. They always want more but are almost never willing to really WORK for it, just on the feet and backs of others.

Now I am sounding too serious and getting off track. After all, this is a fun book. Let's face it, thinking scares bosses because you may think how much better you can do somewhere else, or how easy it would be to sue them, or how you could kill them and hide the body without a trace. We have all had those thoughts, but we (most of the time) think about them and laugh them off. I, on the other hand, say hogwash and tell them just what's on my mind, rather than waste it on my wife or child or a poor unsuspecting neighbor. After a famous person once said, "If you don't want to hear the answer, then don't ask the question." So I do so with great gusto and full knowledge that at anytime this boss could fire me. But that's the chance you take to have an independent thought and express it from time to time. I am never disrespectful at first, but if the boss doesn't respect me, why should I respect them? You or I are not a lesser person just because we are not bosses. As a matter of fact I have been a manager once, and I know of what I speak. (But I was not a boss.) But that's just me, and I am sure there are others that feel as I do and welcome the chance for a verbal meeting of the minds.

So now, at last, to the question: "What did you do it like that for?" Hmmmm…Now this is another good question they already know but want you to give them an answer that they can ruin you with. If you act like this is a scary thing, you will lose as I have said in the past. A calm, cool exterior will see you through every time. Chances are if whatever it was that you did messed up then you will be a little nervous to start with, but you still should be calm and maintain.

Peter Shelton

Chapter 3

Well, buddy, if you think you can do better than this, you do it.

You can bet after a few times of this kind of banter you can be
sure that I have heard this line before. This is an attempt to show you
who is in charge and that you are just a low peon to be trampled. So
after you baffle them they want to get nasty and threaten. But we can
handle that. After all, you and I were the ones to get them to this
point to start with. This is a line along the same line as "I'll take my
ball and go home wah wah." This is an insult to our intelligence and
to our self-esteem. The low brow that told me this is like no other I
have ever seen before or since. (Thank god) This person was in good
shape, wore expensive jewelry, drove a new fine car, and made about
$80,000 + per year. But through all this had two rotten teeth in the
front and would pass gas as loudly as they could and laugh about it
when no one was around. They wanted to impress and also be an
extreme sexist. This is the kind of person that told me this line, "Well,
buddy, if you can do better, you do it." I had to laugh at this poor
excuse for an example of the human race. As we talked about earlier,
this is still their own language talking, or as we said, "Boss terms."
They really don't want you to do better, they just want to scare you
into submission. These kinds of bosses don't want to think or act with
a reasonable amount of intelligence. They just want results and don't
care how they get them. All they ever want is the job done and don't
care who or what they must do to get it whether it is to scare you,
harass you, rattle your cage, or fire you and find some other poor soul
that they can intimidate. Never, never, never be intimidated by any
boss. For one main reason, you were looking when you found this
job, and there always other jobs around the corner that would
appreciate you much more than one that has a boss like this. But 9
out of 10 times they won't fire you. They are the ones that need you
more than you need them. But even if they do, there's not much here
with a boss like this. Trust me, been there done that. And I hope I
will never have a boss like this again. They don't want you to do

better; they want you to roll over and beg for forgiveness, and that's something I will never do. After all, it is just a job and nothing more.

The time that this question or statement came about I was loading a truck, and this boss came out and told me just how lucky I was to work here and how great the business was. I tried to just keep smiling and keep my mouth shut, but when he came to the "How great business was," I asked him then about a raise. I was told, "Well, you are being paid. What more do you want?" So I came back with, "(I named the competition) is making this amount." That's when this statement came about. It would have not come out of me, but I was making about $5 an hour less than the whole industry, and this person was telling me only after the last review that we were so broke, that now we were doing so great and how much money we were now making. My last review stated that I was a great employee, and I would go far if I kept it up, but at this time there was no money for a raise. So that's how this statement came up. I had the nerve to talk back to a boss and make sense at the same time. (Something they are not used to) I know I should have kept my mouth shut, but I was getting tired of hearing about this boss's new car and their new summer house by the lake and such, when I was just keeping my head above water.

So I taunted them a little. Who could blame me? This boss made it a point to let everyone know just how much they were worth and how many possessions they had, not that I would ever deny anyone of being successful, but after awhile of hearing about it and having my nose rubbed into it, I got a little miffed. Here is an example of OLE rotten tooth's idea of a morning conversation.

Boss: Good morning. I had laser surgery done on my eyes last night.

Me: Oh yeah? I have heard of that. I was thinking about that for myself.

Boss: Oh, well, it is very expensive. I don't think you can afford it, and our insurance will not cover it in any way, shape, or form. You have to have the money up front.

As I said, rubbing our noses in it all the time. I didn't feel guilty about telling what part of my body to kiss. So when this came up I also didn't feel guilty about answering this statement either. And as you might have figured out, I did answer them also.

Question: "Well, buddy, if you can do better than this, you just do it."

Some more answers that will ruin their day, but brighten yours.

1) That's what my spouse keeps saying.
2) What and miss out on all my benefits?
3) I did try to go to (name of their competition), but they said since I worked here, I was ruined.
4) What and miss out on your smiling face?
5) Does this mean you're mad about something?
6) What and miss out on seeing your red faced?
7) You go first.
8) Only if you give me a good letter of recommendation.
9) I would, but that would mean higher pay and that would throw me into a higher tax bracket.
10) What and miss out on the chance to be your boss?
11) What and give up a place that cares about their employees so much?
12) Naw...... Thank you anyway, but I would rather stay here and be the pain in your side.
13) How could I ever do better than this? (Then start laughing)
14) My, you are anal-retentive today, aren't you?
15) Then who would you abuse?

Out of these answers will breed many other different types of statements, some of which are these:
"Since when do the employees talk to their employers like that?"
Or "Since when do the employees tell the employer what to do?"
Or "Since when do the employees know more than the employer?"
This is one where they are just begging for an answer.

These are the most common. They don't care what your opinion is; they just want to run off at the mouth, and they do. A lot. When you have a boss such as the one here that i had the most displeasure to work for, they will do everything they can to use and abuse you. And they think that they are doing you a favor by pointing out your every error and every misgiving and short-coming whether they are at work or in your home life. But the gate can swing both ways. I say, if they are going to dish it out, then they can take it." These weak-minded people are just itching for a fight and won't leave anyway until you give them one. When they start this up, why not give them one and win while you're at it.

Let's start with the first question: "Since when do the employees talk to their employer like that?" Bosses don't want you to talk to them. They just want yes men and women. Say yes to everything they want and don't give them any trouble about it. So let us come back at them like this.

Quick witted answers:

1) You should come around to the break room and hear what we say.
2) Sorry, your holiness, I forgot.
3) Every time you turn around. I just forgot to wait until you did this time.
4) Who do you think you are? The grand inquisitor?
5) Well I am trying to start a new trend.
6) Hold on. Let's see if that's covered in the handbook.
7) Not very observant, are you?
8) Employees, customers, strangers, anyone who walks in off the street......
9) Why? Who called you an asshole this time?
10) Anyone who ever had to work for you, I am willing to bet.
11) Are you kidding? Even your computer laughs at you.
12) I was just trying to show some initiative.
13) Not a good listener, are you?
14) You better have your hearing checked.
15) Since you have been in charge.

16) It is a new company policy. Didn't you get the fax?

Question number 2:

Since when do the employees tell the employer what to do?

Some more answers that will leave them stunned

1) Ever since you have been in charge. (Yes this one works here also)
2) Someone has to tell you what to do. You can't find the bathroom by yourself.
3) We wouldn't have to if you knew what it is you were talking about in the first place.
4) Don't you have an animal to abuse or something?
5) You need to get a life. You know that, don't you, or am I stepping out of line again by telling you what to do?
6) What? You're not used to someone who can make full sentences?
7) We have been for years, and you thought you got to where you are by yourself?
8) That's where all your ideas come from, so why not?
9) Quit your job......Damn! Didn't work. You're still here.
10) Since when do you listen to us anyway?
11) Someone here has to have a good thought. You sure as hell don't.
12) Are you kidding? This is where you steal the good ideas from and take credit for it. 13) Since you say I tell you what to do......then go to hell.
13) 9:00 A.M. Sir only when I am on the clock.
14) Does this mean I will get your raise for thinking for you?

Question 3: Since when do the employees know more than the employer?

More answers to befuddle them.

1) Is this a trick question?
2) On whose back did you get to where you are?
3) We do the work, you take the credit, so that would be "always."
4) Not only do we know more, we do more.
5) Since when do you need to ask such an asinine question?
6) Since when do we not?
7) Doesn't take a brain surgeon to beat you out in knowledge.
8) Oh I forgot. I is a dumb OLE worker.
9) Are you kidding? I bet you can't even set your VCR.
10) Why? You still having trouble pushing that pull door and need help?
11) Why? You need help with the difference between the restroom and the closet again?
12) I would be surprised if I didn't know more than you.
13) I would say when you bought that equipment that was outdated 15 years ago because "You got a good deal."
14) Let's see what day did we all start?
15) At least you have people you can steal ideas from so you can keep your position.

These will lead into even more banter that will amaze you as to how your boss even got here to start if you have one such as this type of boss. And it will be fun along the way. Always remember keep cool even when they yell or scream at you. This means you are winning, and they have no other recourse but to resort to a yelling match.

But be above that. Be above yelling. Just smile a lot. That way they can't really fire you because you are not losing your cool. You never want to climb down to their level and yell back. That means they win and the game is over, and we are just getting started here. Be calm, be fun loving, but don't back down either. Show them you won't take this lying down. Poke a little fun at them. After all, they started all this. You're along for the ride.

Peter Shelton

Chapter 4 (this is a short chapter)

How to answer the phone when you realize your boss is on the other end.

Yes, we cover everything in this book, including, but not limited to, this subject. Here you are at home sick or sore or maybe hurt or maybe you just need a break from work for a day. Then the ringing of the phone disturbs your peace and quiet. And you don't have an answering machine, and you think maybe it is important, and you should answer it. After all it may be Aunt Clara or Uncle Pete or someone else who you may want or need to talk to. So you bite your nails and answer it and guess who? Yep, it is the boss wondering why you are at home. It's not enough that these knuckle-draggers bother you at work. Now they are calling you at home and giving you grief. If you are just an average person and not someone who takes a lot of time off for no reason, they should not bother you, but they do anyway. (And if you miss more work than you are at work, chances are that you change jobs a lot anyway) So here you are in an uncomfortable position trying not to sweat over the phone talking to your boss and answering them as to why you are at home.

Just because you had temperature of 101 degrees, why didn't you come in today and work? Amazing, isn't it? You're at home now feeling like you did some major crime in your own home by someone you don't like to start with, for not going to work and either infecting everyone else, or because of pain or maybe just because you needed a break before you strangled someone. Well I have a few ways to cure this. Also, as you might have guessed, and as always, everything in this book I have used and I have had happened to me at one point or another. So these are all true, and they all work. Trust me. I have done all of these at one time or another, and I hate to say it, but the bosses are too inept to figure it out.

Phone Rings: Hello, this is (boss's name)

Answers that will miff them.

1)   You say "Hello," wait a few seconds after you know who it is, then go "HAHA! Fooled you. I am not home. Please leave your name and number after the beep......Beep

2)   Hello: after you know who it is...use an accent of your choice: "What do you want? Who is this? I do not know who this is. I am sorry. You must have the wrong number." Then hang up

3)   Hello: after you find out who it is... "I can't hear you. Anyone there? Speak up. Hello. Hello." Then hang up. The next day make it a point to tell everyone about a obscene phone call you had while you were off sick and make sure it gets back to the boss. They will not say that they were the one that called you.

4)   Hello: after you know who it is......"I can't talk. I have explosive diarrhea."

5)   Hello: after you know who it is... Just hang up and turn the phone ringer off. It will still ring on their side, but you won't be bugged by it.

6)   Hello: after you know who it is......Start lowering or raising your voice and say, "No, they are not awake right now. They are in bed sick. This is their (some relative). Can I take a message?"

7)   Hello: after you know who it is...Put the phone down by the TV and turn it up and turn it to the education channel. Maybe they will learn something from some puppet.

8)   Hello: after you know who it is......Turn the tables on them; ask them if they are calling on company time?

9)   Hello: after you know who it is...This one needs explaining first. We had a boss that always said we spent too much time on the phone whether it was for taking orders or for sales, and on our breaks and lunches we spent way too much time on the phone, and they could listen in to any conversation they want to. So they sent out a letter that we were only allowed 2.9 minutes on the phone and that was even for the sales staff. So back to the phone call now. Hello: after you know who it is. "Make it

quick. We are allowed 2.9 minutes on the phone, and I am recording this conversation for posterity."

10)   Hello: after you know who it is. "What the hell do you want? Isn't it enough I made myself sick to do my job so well that I had to stay home today and recuperate?"

11)   Hello: after you know who it is..."Wrong number." Then take the phone off the hook and tell them you were on the computer.

12)   Hello: after you know who it is...Make static noises in the mouth piece and tell them to call back. Then turn the phone off.

13)   Hello: after you know who it is... Ask them if this is how they spend their time when they should be working.

14)   Hello: after you know who it is......Start gagging on the phone like you're going to throw up and hang up. They won't call back.

15)   Hello: after you know who it is...Act like they woke you up from trying to rest from being sick and get a little irritated in the conversation. Say sorry a lot and explain to them it is from being tired and sick.

Now the next day you will hear from your boss, and there are statements that will flow from them like sewerage from a pipe that broke. The main statement will be along the lines like: "You're missing too many days from work." (It could be only two days. It wouldn't matter, and in chapter 10 we will go in more depth.) So be ready for it and remember keep your cool.

"We are monitoring this phone conversation":

At one place I worked they would listen in to your phone calls whether you called out or someone called in to you. I know it is their phone, and they pay the bills, but there are ways to keep the long distance calls from happening other than being a "Peeping tom" to your phone calls. Some bosses are just starved for entertainment. I guess they have no excitement in their life so they must intrude into yours. These are one of the lowest forms of bosses next to an amoeba. But I was at a place that did that all the time, and not tell you that they were doing it, and then use it against you later with the recording of your conversation. Nice huh? There was a room at the top of the stairs that they would monitor the phones. So as you well know by now from reading this book I would be the thorn in their side. There would be many times that I would throw a smoke bomb into it, or take a padlock and lock them into the room and such things like this just so they knew that I was around (but could never prove it). There are many ways to beat this. Also, you can't get them through a lawyer because, as I said, it is their phone, but there are other ways you can make their ears burn so that they will not want to listen in on you. Like I have been saying, I have done them all. I know at least most of them work.

One way is to have someone call you when you know someone else is "online" and have them talk dirty to you. This will have at least four effects:

1) They will be so bored by your other calls, they will not listen.
2) They will be so shocked that they will never listen in again.
3) They will confront you about it, then you can ask them why they were listening to my phone calls. This will embarrass them. Ask them if they are a pervert.
4) Or they will just blush and leave you alone.

Or another way is if you hear the click of someone else "online," you can blow a whistle. Another way is to start talking to your boss as if you know they are there, start asking them their opinion. (The only bad thing about this one is since they know, it all they just may tell you.) Or the OLE fashioned way, ask them just who is listening in on my phone call on my break time. There are a lot of ways you can get this effect, but these will be in another book. This is a short chapter, and I need to move on. I still have a lot of ground to cover.

Chapter 5

"Are you doing that on company time?"

Now let's look into the mind of a boss for a while. We looked at their language. Now let's try to think like them for a while. Here you are, you just had a really hard 4 hours, and you go to the bathroom or go and get a soda or a snack. Just then a boss crawls out and sees you. They haven't been spotted all day, but as soon as you get up or go to get a drink, they are right behind you. Now instead of just saying hello, they start in with their usual dribble about what are you doing, or this one, which is a lot different but sounds the same to us lay people: "Are you doing that on company time?"

Now by definition "What are you doing?" means they don't know what you are doing because they are not observant enough to figure it out or too stupid or lazy. "Are you doing that on company time?" means that they know what you are doing, and they want to know if they are losing money on you while you do whatever you are doing when they see you. And it is worlds apart by a boss's way of thinking (if that's what you want to call what goes on in their heads). Like I said, back to the question. These people have a sixth sense about what they think is their money leaving their pockets and someone that they think is getting paid for nothing. They are like a dog sniffing out a bone. They know when it is time to walk out and mess with people. I have a fellow worker that would work his butt off. He was a go-getter, but every time, and I do mean every time (we used to joke about it), he would go and get a cup of coffee, or go smoke, or go to the bathroom, the boss would be out looking for him. He was fired once (but rehired) for smoking in the back of a trailer that was pulled away from the building. Now, as the story goes, I was a truck driver at the time. It was winter, and everyone that smoked asked me to pull a trailer away from the door so that they had a dry spot to smoke. Now this was four feet from the dock, and we were not using that trailer that day so everyone used it for a smoking lounge, until this fellow went into it. Now when the boss saw him they fired him saying that "This is a extension of the building" Don't ask me. I didn't get it either, but the boss fired him anyway. When I got back, I found out what had happened. So I asked, "What the hell did you fire him for? I was told the tale, and I started laughing. I then told the boss that the trailer was not touching the building at all and that I had pulled it out of the door because we were not using it, and everyone had been in there including his boss to smoke. The fellow was rehired the next day. But some of us have luck like that, and we have to deal with it and are forced to answer questions like "Are you doing that on company time?"

One of my answers is always, "Yes, I am sir!" But that's me. I guess I am just a little different. I was once told I have moxy. (Or just no brains. I haven't figured out which one yet.) Either way it somehow works for me. Another example of "Are you doing that on company time?" is you just got done with a long drawn out project, and you sit down for a minute to have a smoke or get a soda or whatever. Here comes your boss, huffing and puffing about you taking a break. Now all these examples have happened at one point or another in my life of dealing with these bosses, and so has my wife and as well as friends of both of us. Any way you're there even after they know what you have been doing all day and the question comes up "Are you doing that on company time?" All you want to do at that point is kick them in the knee and yell YES! But being a well-rounded person and a good sport, you just smile and try to tell them what you were doing all day. Or on the other hand if you're a little me, you smile and answer them and tell them in your own way just what is on your mind.

Question: "Are you doing that on company time?"

The list continues of quick replies:

1) 1) Yes, why? Jealous?
2) No, I am doing this on my time. You're just paying me for it.
3) No, I am doing this on borrowed time from my neighbor.
4) Why not? Ii do work for you on my time.
5) Why are you asking? Bored or something??
6) Doing what?

7) No, I am not really here. I am really over there.
8) Must......Rest......Need......Break......
9) Maybe......Maybe not.
10) What? Did you hear the sound of my candy wrapper?
11) Imagine what you could do if only you thought about what you say.
12) You need new material.
13) No, I am taking back the extra minute I gave you last week that I didn't get paid for.
14) No, I am talking to you on company time though.
15) You bet. I love to get by with anything I can. I lie, cheat, steal, and everything (this answer will more then likely just stun them).

And, of course, this will span as always other things they will try to do to you like, "Ok then maybe we will just fire you, or maybe just get back to work, or there are ten others that will love to have this job or a verbal or written warning." I never have understood the mind of a boss. I mean I know how it thinks, but as to why it works the way it does, is beyond me. So I don't try. I just know which way the chips will fly and how to either duck or throw them right back at them.

They think that most people are just plain stupid or just have no backbone when in truth it is the bosses that are the ones that have no sense to tie their own shoe. Here is another example of a brain dead boss. My old boss at one company used to walk through the plant and just fire people just to see their reaction. Well one day he walked up to a person and said, "You are fired. Get out of my building." Well this person just looked up at him and said in these words, "I don't work for you asshole." The boss replied, "oh, you don't work for me?" "No, I was one of your customers until this point. Now you can just cancel my order."

Leap before you look is what bosses do best, and that was just one time. He also fired some truck driver that didn't work for him and a city worker who came in to check the gas or water or something. You would think that that after the first time this boss might have learned, but we are talking about a boss after all. So that leaves that theory right out. This boss also thought that no matter how much you did, no matter how many hours you put in, that was never enough, and you could do more. We had this fellow that worked at this place once who had a car wreck, a bad one. This poor guy was in a coma for about 3 weeks, and instead of being concerned about his well being, he said, "He is just sucking money out of me." This boss went to the hospital to tell the doctors to wake him up because he couldn't afford the bill anymore. You may think this is a limited view of what really happens in the wonderful world of work, but trust me, it happens everyday in the real world of jobs and bosses. Here is one sad example of what can happen. I knew one fellow that had an injury to his knee, and the morning earlier he took aspirin because his knee was sore. Well later that day he slipped on some oil that was left by a forklift and went to the company doctor. He was refused because it was a "preexisting condition." He went through the whole gambit and took it to court and asked the company lawyer this question, "Do you mean to tell me if i had a headache in the morning, and I took aspirin for it, and I had say a 71 pound box of tile fall on my head, that would be a preexisting condition?" The lawyer said in front of the judge "yes," and the company won the suit.

That's the real way bosses think of their employees. But now we are becoming too serious, and this is one thing this book is not going to do for very long. We have a lot of ground to cover so let us continue.

"Isn't your break over yet?"

Now who in their right mind would answer yes to this one while you are sitting down, or outside smoking a cigarette, or whatever you may do on break? Well they still ask this question once in a while. As dumb as it sounds, it happens. Or a variation of this is "these 20 minutes breaks are killing us." Or "I wish I had as many breaks as you people do." There are many, many others, but for now we will stick to the one that started all this. "Isn't your break over with yet?" Just like the other question, "Are you doing that on company time?" they know when your breaks are and know when you should be working. They just want to mess with you. They all think, as I have stated, you are stealing their money, and if you aren't moving then they shouldn't pay you. Bosses wouldn't let you have a break or a lunch if they could get out of it. Their idea of a good employee is a machine that never quits, unless of course they pick it out, and it was a piece of junk to start with. Now I am getting ahead of myself.

Most people don't take any longer than they are allotted for break and don't take longer for lunches. Now I did say most people. There are always those others that the Bosses are right about but who never get caught. But we always do, don't we. Didn't see the person that ran a forklift off the dock but can spot you taking 45 seconds extra on a break or lunch. (And yes this has also happened) I think I like the look on their faces when they ask these questions. I guess that is my favorite part of this entire book, the look on their faces before you answer them, and of course, after.

Question: "Isn't your break over with yet?"

10 answers that will insure that look we all love to see.

1) (No matter what time you started it) No sir, I started late. (Then smile at them)
2) I will answer that question......after my break.
3) This is my time unless you want to pay me for it. Go away.
4) Hold on. Let me clock back in if I am going to match wits with you again.
5) No, sir, I am not management. I don't get two-hour lunches and one-hour breaks.
6) Well if I am, you of all people should be able to tell; your whole job is a break.
7) Yes about two hours ago. Why?
8) I'm sorry I can't hear you on my time. Otherwise I would have to tell you to kiss my ass. (This means yes I am still on break by the way)

9) Ask the boss a question that you know they will give you a 20-minute explanation for then when they are done you will have extended your time.
10) Nope, I am taking a siesta.
11) Sure is, but I wanted to hear you yell again.
12) Sure I am. Just wanted to see if you were paying attention.
13) Nope, my whole job is a break. Remember, you yourself told me that.
14) I'm not on break. I am sitting here thinking about how to do my job better.
15) Yep, it sure is. What's your point?

Any of these answers will get that look going, and the fun will start. The game is on!

Chapter 6

"The Company Snitch"

We all know someone or some people that if you pass gas on company time, they run you over to the boss. (A manager doesn't need a snitch and often tells them to get out of here.) The kind we had at one of my jobs was a screwball. He would tear up so much equipment and freight because he was always rushing to impress the boss that it became a running joke. But he would always blame someone else. And to top things off, if you so much as sneezed, he would accuse you of beating time and report it. To give you a idea of this bozo, he ran a forklift into 17 dock doors, turned over a fork lift, cut off his own finger by showing someone how "Not to run a cutting machine," turned over a truck because he said a pack of wild animals of some sort ran out in front of him, backed a trailer into a car, the car into a dumpster and the car and dumpster into a wall, then coming out of the repair shop with the truck that he turned over after just getting fixed, cut the corner too sharply and tore the front end of a tractor trailer off. Well, you get the idea. But yet kept his job for 27 years because he was a true blue snitch.

Oh, by the way, a snitch is by definition: 1) Always, I repeat ALWAYS, rushing but never gets anything done then blames you for it; 2) Always showing you the right way to do something but either screws up or takes twice as long to do it their way (then blames you for it); 3) Unsafe in any environment, but tells everyone that it is you that don't know what you're doing; 4) Even though this freak of nature does all of this and more, they are the ones who run and report you to the boss about the least little things to take attention away from themselves. Even your bathroom habits aren't safe around this creature of darkness. (How often and how much time it takes the one I had carried a stopwatch)

By the way I am comparing this to a warehouse situation, but we all have had these types of people among us. The snitch is a modern mystery of society by all means. They have to work with you all day but run into the boss to tell on you. Waa Waa Waa! They will sit and stare at you for hours just to wait for you to mess up, even though while they are watching you they are doing no work. That is beside the point. Strange but true, my friends, the snitch in our place went to the boss and told on us one day. It was winter; we were loading customers, and the dock door was open. Well the customer left, but we forgot to shut the dock door. It was not a really cold day so no one noticed. Well the snitch went to the boss and said and I quote: "I have been sitting here on my lift for two hours right here in this spot, and no one closed that dock door, and it has been letting out the heat." Now all in all we did leave it open. It was not that cold, but we were working, NOT SITTING STARING AT A DOOR for two hours. The snitch decided to tell the boss. This too was a good person; he was a manager, not a boss, and he asked the snitch, "well why didn't you close it yourself?" He said, "I didn't leave it open." The manager then asked, "How do you know it was open for two hours? They might have closed it and opened it for someone else?" Snitch: "NO. NO. I didn't move. I was right here." The manager then said, "Well if you were here then you were not working. So get back to it NOW!!!"

We all loved it. Laughter rang through the place. This was the first time in 20 years the snitch messed up and stuck his foot in his mouth. He has had a few fists in there also, but that is another story.

The snitch has two phrases they may use on you at any given time which we will address right now.

The first phrase is, "let me show you the right way to do it. I've been here for x-amount of years. The second is, "I'm telling (insert bosses name here)."

Let's look at the first one and go from there.

Phrase: Let me show you the right way to do it. I've been here for x-amount of years.

Answers that should confuse them which won't take much.

1) Not just no but HELL NO.
2) No, you do it your way which has been wrong for x-amount of years.
3) Please don't. I still owe the doctor from the last time you showed me how to do it the "Right way."
4) Go ahead. I need a good laugh.
5) Call everyone over to watch and laugh.
6) If it is the right way then why are YOU showing me?
7) Go ahead. After they show you, have them do it about 3 or 4 more times, and act like you are really watching. It is a good way to kill a few hours.
8) Run away screaming.
9) Go to the medicine cabinet and bring out Band-Aids just in case.
10) Start yawning and find somewhere to sit down.
11) Do you know a right way to jump out of a four story window then ask them to show you by doing it.
12) "Since when did the right way ever stop you from doing anything?"
13) Well that would be a first for you
14) Why? Did you just learn yourself?
15) They are not letting you breed, are they?

Phrase number two: "I'm telling the boss."

Answers that should exorcise this demon.

1) I'm surprised they can understand you seeing as your nose is so far up their ass.
2) Make sure you pronounce my name right for a change.
3) Be sure to put your kneepads on before you assume the position.
4) Be sure to show them the itemized bill for all the things you damaged when you were trying to show me the right way to use it.

5) OOOOOOOO for the millionth time.
6) Fine, and I'll call the president.
7) Need directions to the office?
8) Go ahead. My forehead still has footprints on it from the last time you did.
9) Your lips must be sore all the time from kissing ass so much.
10) Big surprise.
11) While you're at it, tell them for me that you're nuts.
12) How can you talk to the boss and kiss ass at the same time?
13) The boss already knows that you're an idiot. What more do you want to tell them?
14) Why not tell the president of the company, or better yet, call the owner. It is a slow day. Maybe they need a good laugh also.
15) Good idea. Show me the right way to act like a moron.

These kinds of answers won't deter the demon from going to the boss, but it sure will be fun saying them. No matter what you would have done, they will go to the boss anyway. And after all, work is just a game, far better to have a little fun and not take it so seriously, or else you might end up a disgruntled employee and aerate your boss with a machine gun or something. And sometimes snitches are fun to be around because they are so stupid to watch them watch you. They watch you through the racks at clothes shops, or through a rack at a warehouse, or behind a door at an office, or on hidden camera. No one is safe from the snitch, not even a boss. Why, the snitch has even turned in a boss to another higher boss that I have seen. I guess he thought that by turning in the boss that he would get the job. Yeah right! What happens is that the boss is fired and the position is done away with to save the company money. Now you have the boss that this snitch went to as the boss over everyone. That is even worse. They are underpaid and overworked now because of the snitch who got the other lesser boss fired under him. Now they have to do their work as well as the other boss's work. So the snitch didn't do anyone any favors.

The snitch comes in all shapes and sizes and backgrounds and so forth. You never know when or where one might be. They just crawl out from under a rock sometimes. Our boss at one time hired a snitch just to watch us and let him know what we did. "A Company spy." Which around a bunch of union people was kind of dangerous for the snitch. He would come out and watch us so intently that no work was being done by him so we just kind of figured out what reason that this person was here for. For example: I was doing some work in a middle section of the warehouse. Well the demon was on a forklift and watching me so intensely that he ran into a concrete pole. Now that wouldn't be so bad except that he had a load on the lift, a 15 foot roll of vinyl. Now he also had a bad habit of driving real fast so when the vinyl ran into the pole, it broke in half. (It is real brittle in the winter.) SO as I was laughing, he took the goods back to stock both pieces and told the manager that it came in damaged. The worse part was that they believed him.

Well, I never said management was intelligent, did i? There are lots of ways to handle snitches. The first thing is to determine which type you have. There are 3 types of snitches:

Type 1: The "you are my pal and buddy" type that will go right after they pat you on the back and report you.

Type2: The loud mouth that will tell you that they will go to the boss.

Type3: The one who acts like a moron and knows nothing about anything.

The first type is easy to spot. They pat you on the back, or kid around with you, or just try to act like one of the gang. Don't be fooled. Always keep your guard up around these fools. We had a spy at one of our places. He would act like he was the life of the party but then ask us questions about the other people. It was as if he was laughing one second then switched to, "Well what do you think of that?" Then ask other questions like that. Not too hard to spot.

The second type, well that's a gimme. We all have had bosses like that.

Third type is the hard one to spot. We had one of those also, the moron spy. They act like nothing bothers them or don't care or are too dumb to worry about it. He was called in to observe a manager that the main bosses thought was neglecting their duties. So this idiot one day runs a forklift into a wall, walks into this person's office, and says, "The forklift is on fire" and walks out real calm. The manager calls the fire department and then the main boss. The main boss came downstairs and ran out to the warehouse. Unknown to this snitch at the time the forklift WAS on fire and burning. Well to make a long tale short, the fire was put out, and the next day the snitch went to the main boss and gave his report.

He told this boss that the manager didn't act fast enough to insure safety. Well this snitch was not only fired, but he was docked his pay to replace the damage to the building and the forklift because the main boss said, "You should have seen the lift on fire, and no one is worth burning the building down just to spy on someone."

And, by the way, it also was five feet from a fire extinguisher.

"Don't you want to advance in this company?"

Hmmm now if you have read this far, you know that with bosses like this the chances of advancing are slim to none. This is just another form of boss language that doesn't make sense, not saying that much of it does anyway, but be that as it may, how many times have you heard this line? It can come delivered to you in many ways,

"Don't you want to advance in this company?" "This is not the way to advance in this company." "There are ways to advance in this company, but this isn't one of them."

There are many more ways to say the same thing. What's funny is they think they are tricking us into believing that we may get advanced! I know better. Maybe with a manager this could happen but not one of the bosses like we have discussed here in this book. The type of bosses in this book try to guilt you into being a better employee and gets more out of you. They use it like a club and beat you over the head with this phrase. But if you're like me it doesn't work. For one thing with the type of bosses and jobs like we have discussed why would you want to advance? You know down in your heart that you will never advance anyway I have tried and tried. I had a job where I did everything they wanted above and beyond the call of duty. It didn't help. All I was told was "good job," and when I asked about getting that advancement I was promised, I was told "We can't afford the luxury of another person being in charge of anything." Ok that was fine. I understood until I found out that once again the boss took all the credit for what I did, and he got the raise and the pat on the back.

Even that would not have upset me as much as finding out that I was the one who did all the planning, all the work, and this boss got the glory. That hurt, and I didn't forget that line about advancing. Now don't get me wrong. A hard day of work still pays off when you have a manager who worked their way up or who appreciates hard work. But when you have a boss, it can backfire.

Now I was doing all the work added to my own duties with the same pay scale. It was now just expected of me to do so because I did it before. So when I couldn't keep up doing all of it, I was let go. Even though the boss knew there was no way I could keep up, he felt threatened by the fact that someone else could do their job as well or better than they did it. And when they told the main manager that I was let go it showed that it was because I could not keep up with the "fast pace aspect of this business."

That is what bothered me the most. But by the same token when I went to another company and did the same thing again, I was advanced, but I had a manager this time, and it worked out wonderfully. So it can backfire if you have a boss.

So to the question at hand if you have a boss who uses this line on you, here are so retaliations you may use.

"Don't you want to advance in this company?"

Some more answers that will shut them up

1) Why? Did Satan quit?
2) Advance to what? Head washroom attendant?
3) Let me think. Advance to the head of a sinking ship. I think not.
4) I'd like to advance myself right to another job.
5) Would that mean I could clear poverty pay?
6) Isn't the boss over the commodes taken?

7) How does one advance in a company moving backwards?
8) No, I like being the company scapegoat.
9) Sure. Do I get paid more, or do you get my raise?
10) Not if it means more work. I need my rest too.
11) Who did you fire this time?
12) Now who quit?
13) Sure I want to be your boss so I can fire you.
14) Why would I want to advance here when the fast food industry offers so much more?
15) Why do you ask? Do you need someone else to take the blame?

And it's not like you're surprising them with these answers. After all, have you ever heard ask a stupid question, get a stupid answer? They just hand you the ammo to shoot them down and run around with a target on their back. I was never one to be able to resist such easy prey. It just comes up to you and leaves itself open for rebutting. And like a lot of animals that are prey, not too smart. So the next time one of these questions come up about advancing in the company, remember it is all a head game.

Chapter 7

It's not broken. You just don't know what the hell you're doing!

Once again they come up with a statement that boggles the mind. "No maybe that piece dangling from there is supposed to be letting out sparks by the fuel tank!" Sometimes these people just leave their brains in a meeting (which we will cover later). Yes sir, I do know how to use a broom, but the handle is in two pieces. Or yes sir I would back up that truck if it still had reverse. Or yes I would go and start the truck, but I need a hill so I can pop start it. It's just amazing what comes out of the holes under their noses someday.

They don't want to spend the money to get it fixed. All they want is...yes, BOTTOM LINE! Never mind that the printer and the computer need an incentive to work (a well placed kick in the software). It's not broken; you need training on how to use it, not we need a new one, but YOU need training. I say, Yes I do. I don't know how to use a piece of junk so please train me. Show me what part I should use the hammer on to get it to work right.

Then we are right back to the statement, "Oh, you're a smart ass!" Well it seems like you can't win so why try, right? If something is broken, show them what it is, where it is, and how much money they lose from it not working right. Hit them where it hurts: productivity! If they still don't want to deal with it or try to fix it, my book wasn't for nothing. It proves my point about bosses. If he has a superior, tell them about it. Who knows? Maybe you too can become a manager someday. Then you can ask your old boss, "Are you working?"

Question: "It's not broken. You just don't know what the hell you're doing."

Even more comebacks to curl their hair.

1) Ok then just add more tape to it, right?
2) Then you show me how to use it. I'll stand over there.
3) So it should shoot sparks at us? (Depending on the situation)
4) You're right. My training never covered how to use a piece of junk like this.
5) Ok, you're right. It is not broken, and you're not a cheapskate.
6) You're right. I don't know what I am doing. I work here, don't I?
7) You wouldn't know what's broken anyway. Hell, you try to push open the pull door.
8) I should have expected as much from someone who can't work the coffeepot.
9) So it should be in more than one piece?
10) You know for some reason that statement doesn't surprise me. (Then just walk away)
11) Yeah, what do I know? I have only used this thing for X-amount of years.
12) For someone who is in your position, you're not very bright, are you?
13) And you do?
14) Sorry. Is the procedure kick it then smack, or smack it then kick it?
15) You're right. I need a bigger bat to convince it to work right.

As you well know this will spawn another question, and of course, you may guess what it will be. "What did you do to it?" You know, it's bad enough you have to use this piece of garbage, but then to listen to this tripe besides, it's enough to warrant pulling your hair out. You use this piece of junk, and it breaks because of lack of maintenance or the tape that held it together gave way. Of course it broke because of something you did to it! It broke because they should have replaced it ten years ago.

To give you a few examples, we had a mainframe computer that took up a 30 foot by 20-foot room. My personal computer at home had more memory. It had a bigger hard drive. Let's face it, a reel to reel computer is a bit outdated. Then we had a truck that had 850,000 miles on it and was falling apart, so they trade it for another tractor that had 1,038,000 miles. Like they told us, they got a good deal on it. Nothing like going from bad to worse, but hey, what do I know? The place that sold us this piece of crap truck saw us coming. It passed an inspection with a bad air brake, the rear axle rocking in the cradle from no U-bolts, and the drive shaft was bad as was the fifth wheel. No way, and I mean NO way, should that truck should have been on the road in that condition. Oh, I forgot, it also had no heat and the tires were bald. Now when I had to drive it for the first, last, and only time, it of course broke down. The radiator shot craps. Well to make matters worse, I was about 75 miles away and had a trailer and had to be towed. Well the first question I was asked was, "What did you do to it?" Now why did I figure that was going to be the first thing out of their mouth? Well, we got it back to the shop, and here is another fine example of not wanting something right. The radiator was 100% kaputz, and a new one was $5000.00. Well, when they heard that, the Boss said we'll just weld the old one back together. That lasted about 35 miles. Someone else was driving in that time. It came back on a hook again, and again the shop was told to weld it again. This time it lasted a whole month before it blew apart again. Once again, it came back on a hook and to make a long story short, it got a new radiator. In the process, though, it cost the company $9200.00 between the tows, the repair, and the new radiator. So once again my Boss did his best to save the company money and again failed in the long run.

Like I said, I love it when they blame you when these pieces of junk backfire in their face. This leads me into the next question...

Question: "What did you do to it?"

Here you go.

1) I used it. What the hell did you think?
2) I turned it on.
3) Be nice. It's old.

4) What do you expect for an antique?
5) 5 I was getting it ready for the museum.
6) Nothing lasts forever, and the equipment around here is sheer proof of that.
7) It's broken again? I'll get the tape.
8) Nothing. I guess that glue didn't hold. Next time buy the $1.99 stuff.
9) The chewing gum that was holding it together fell off.
10) I threatened to fix it.
11) It was x-amount of years old...get a grip.
12) Nothing. It's been like that for years. Just kick it a few more times. It will work.
13) Nothing. Its get up and go got up and walked out.
14) Nothing...yet.
15) The same thing I have been doing to it for x-amount of years, but today it just didn't like it.

An answer like one of these or more like these will do nicely to shut them up. Not only do I give you answers to use, but also be creative. Invent some of your own. I'm sure that through this whole book there have been a few dog answers, but that is my own way of dealing with bosses. There are many other ways and answers you can use, and as always, say it with a smile!

Chapter 8

You're not allowed to be sick on a Monday or Friday!

No one plans to be sick or hurt. Companies think that we plan to be sick on certain days just to have a 3-day weekend. Now I will agree that some of us do take advantage and will use that for a 3-day weekend, but not everyone does. Most of us know and do the right thing. Most of us know that taking a 3-day weekend is not the right thing to do because of that very reason. Have you ever tried to tell the germs not to get you on Sunday night? (I don't think they know what a time clock is) What happens if you child comes home with a fever of 101? You do your best to avoid them, but for those of us who have kids, we all know one thing: When the child has a fever of 101, it is not as bad as what it would be if we get a fever of 101. How about if you break your arm on Saturday? Do you tell your arm to heal before Monday? A boss thinks that no matter what is wrong, you are just "beating time." A person that does it on a regular basis, I can understand the reaction, but for most of us, we just want to be healthy because no normal person likes to be sick or hurt.

Bosses like we have discussed have their own language and thoughts. They think like a sewer lid: never opened until they have to be. Then once opened it kind of has a stench. They believe that no one but them have an excuse to be ill. How many times have you known a boss to call in on a Monday or Friday? Let's face it. No matter when you are sick, they don't believe you anyway. It's even worse if it is a Monday or Friday. Companies believe that people just want a free ride, and no one wants to work. The idiots that run the joint are the ones who abuse it the most because they can.

I knew of a Boss that wanted to use Comp Time. Comp Time would have worked like this at this place: No overtime for anything less than 80 hours in a two week pay period. This would mean that they could work you up to 80 hours in one week and none the next, or 70 then 10 or 60/20 and so on. No sick time or vacation because you could work more if you wanted to and either cash in the Comp. Time or use it, as it would accumulate. There was a person who went to church and didn't drink or smoke and never went out on Sunday or any holiday. They never worked, and I mean never worked, on a Sunday. Nice, huh? He didn't want to work on a holiday or Sunday but wanted everyone else to so he could make more money and not have to pay extra money for vacations, holidays, or sick time. Oh well. He went out of business shortly after that was implemented because no one wanted to work for him. So my point, sick time, vacation time, and such are something that no Boss wants you to use. So I say use your time whenever you need it. Don't be worried what the next knuckle-dragging Boss says. If you are reading this book, for one thing you have great intelligence and good taste I might add, so I don't think you are the type of person to use it in the wrong way just to get a three-day weekend. So I say use these days and do so with a smile, and if the next time they tell you that you can't be sick on Monday or Friday, I say go into work and cough or throw up on them. For one thing it will get their attention, two it will make you feel better, and three they will send you home, which is where you wanted to be to begin with! Be sure to tell them after you cough or sneeze or puke on them just how contagious you are and any form of contact that they will need to go to their own doctor. It will be fun, and it will be something you can tell your grandkids about.

"You're not allowed to be sick on a Monday of Friday."

Here are even more things to say or do.

1) Ok, I'll tell my germs that.
2) What happens if I do get sick and come in, and you get sick on those days?
3) How about if I call in dead?
4) So if I have a heart attack, should I bring the EKG machine in with me?
5) Ok I'll be here Monday and Friday, but I won't be here Tuesday through Thursday.
6) Come into work and sneeze or cough or puke on them, tell them in a most serious voice how contagious you are, and they should call their own doctor.

7) Just say ok and keep going to get coffee and food and tissues and to the bathroom and so forth. When they ask you what you are doing, just tell them you need to keep eating and drinking because of the medicine, and of course, the bathroom trips are from all that, and you keep sneezing so you need tissues.

8) Tell them that the medicine makes you drowsy and keep falling asleep.

9) Tell everyone around you how sick you are and that the boss won't let you off because it is a Monday or Friday.

10) Act like you may throw up at any minute all day.

11) So if I break my arm, I should come in because I still have one good arm?

12) Should I bring in a mortician's slip if I die from this?

13) Should I have my next of kin call you if I do get worse?

14) Sure I'll come in, and infect everyone else.

15) I'll be here Monday, and I'll be sure to stop by and cough on you along the way.

Onward to other related things: Doctor's slips. If you have a boss like mine, you know that even if they see you the day before and know just how bad you feel, it doesn't matter. If you're off work for more than two days, you had better have one of these or else they think you are just being lazy. They must get a note that you went to a doctor. Now how often have you felt sick but knew it wasn't bad enough to waste your time or the doctor's time to go to their office? If you're like me, I am sure there have been a few. They should thank me for not going. I have insurance through my place of business so when I don't go to the doctor, I save them money. But my boss wants me to go no matter what, so I do, and I make sure I turn in that bill. Some people will, of course, abuse sick days, but as always we are talking about regular people here who don't believe in that. We are the ones that the company counts on but get the shaft. I once had a bad reaction to a medicine, and I called the doctor. He just told me to just stay in bed and I'll be ok and not to take anymore of that medicine. When I called my employer and told them this, it wasn't good enough. I had to have a note. So I risked driving to the doctor and got my note. Afterward the doctor gave me a bit of trouble about driving and told me to go straight home and get back into bed. He wrote me a note for two days instead of one because he thought it was insane for them to make me go all though this. So needless to say, my boss wasn't very happy, but they never are, so who cares. This is the nature of corporate nowadays. They want you at work no matter what. By their way of thinking if you needed cancer treatments once a week or whatever time, you would get fired because you were not at work. I was once told that was the truth of that statement also.

This one boss told me just that. He said it is not a crime to be sick and even though you have been here for 10 years and you need these treatments if you're not at work at your time then you're fired. The family and medical leave act only covers you if you are off for 3 days in a row and if your place of business has 50 employees or more. So tell me what good is that if you need one day off a week for an illness? Oh, well, I think they figure that you can either keep your job and die from lack of treatment or get the treatment and get fired. Either way it doesn't sound good.

So if your boss asks you for a doctor's slip, you can either go to the doctor every time you sneeze, or you can handle it other ways, some of which I mentioned earlier. Moving on to other related things in the Medical field and work Worker's Compensation. Oh this is a part that happened to me, and I am going to love writing this one out. I will get a bit serious for a bit, but I will come back to myself at the end here. You ever get hurt at work and have to go to one of these (and I use the term loosely) Doctors? Well I had the misfortune to be in that group that had to. I pushed off a 900 pound and an 800 pound roll of carpet off a truck by myself. I was young and didn't know any better. I was told that I had to get it off and delivered. So I got it off and tore up my shoulder and lower back.

So I got the chance to go to the Worker's Compensation Doctor. Now everything I have told you so far in this book is 100% true, and this is no exception. Believe it or not, but I have the lawyer's paperwork to back me up on it. Anyway I went into this "Doctor's office" thinking I was in good hands. For starters I was never x-rayed at all. I was given a 20-pound weight limit and was told to go back to work on light duty. So I did, and let me tell you, my company's idea of light duty and mine are far different. They sent me out with 5000 pounds of carpet pad to deliver. So I told my "Doctor" what had happened, and he then put me on a 10-pound weight limit. So the next day my company had me moving trucks around knowing full well that my shoulder and back were hurt. Now there was light work there like writing up the trucks that came in or a bunch of other paperwork that needed to be done. But I was not doing any of that. I was moving trucks. So I told my "Doctor" again what was going on, and he then put me on a five pound weight limit and no driving. Still no x-ray. So when I got back to my job, I handed them the note and was then sent down to cut vinyl on the cutting machine on the six-foot vinyl floor. Now I am on a five pound weight limit, and these six-foot rolls can weigh up to 600 pounds. You have to use a two-wheel dolly to move them, then hoist them up onto the cutting machine. I did it for two days. I called the "Doctor," and he then told me that sometimes companies get into a bind, and they had to use me like that. I should do the best I could. I then called a few federal agencies and asked about all of this. One told me that moving a 900-pound roll and picking it up are two different things. I then told him that I will bring a roll down and for him to show me the different. I was hung up on. The other agency told me to get a lawyer. And the last one told me to call Worker's Comp. I did that also and was told to get a lawyer. Well into the third day of moving six-foot vinyl, I had a 300-pound roll fall on me and pin me down to the concrete floor. I was sent back to the "Doctor." He told me that my hand turning blue and going numb was all in my head, psychosomatic. So I got mad and screamed at them for a few minutes, and at last I was sent to an orthopedic "Doctor."

He x-rayed me and found nothing. I will tell you why this was important here in a sec. He did let me off of work for a week, and I did get a little better. My hand stopped turning blue and going numb. I thought that was a plus. I then went back to work the next week still sore, but I didn't want to mess around with the Worker's Comp "Doctors" anymore. I then had a car wreck; four months later someone hit me. I went to my own Doctor and had my shoulder and back x-rayed. He told me something amazing. My lower back was missing two discs. They just disintegrated. My shoulder had a bundle of pinched nerves, and I was a mess. The car wreck I had wasn't that bad. The only reason I went to the Doctor was because my company told me I had to get a work release. I asked if this could have just did it by itself over time like four months. He said yes and no, but it looked more like a trauma had happened. I then explained what happened to me four months before with Worker's Comp and such. He asked me if the other "Doctor" had told me of the missing discs. I said no; he didn't mention it at all. Imagine that. Now the point of this story, kids, is never, never, never trust a Worker's Comp "Doctor," in my opinion, that is. Always get a second opinion even if you have to pay for it yourself. It's well worth the money. I have 10 rules about Worker's Comp. The first three are real; the rest are ones like don't do what I did rules. I will write out here, and like I said, these are my opinion. With that in mind...

Rule 1) Get a lawyer right off the bat, and keep them informed every day if you have to.
Rule 2) Get a second opinion.
Rule 3) Make notes of everything, and keep all your paperwork.

Now the "don't do what I did" rules:

Rule 4) Never tell the "Doctors" that the only reason they are here is because they couldn't make it in real medicine.
Rule 4) That they all made D's in Medical school.
Rule 5) Don't pull the cabinet off the wall with your good arm.
Rule 6) Don't tell them that the only way you're going to put that needle in me is over my dead body. Remember, this is the person who is giving you the shot and could give you anything.
Rule 7) Don't tell the "Doctors" in front of a full room of patients that they should go down and visit Satan.
Rule 8) Don't ask the nurse, "How's the horse the doctor treated yesterday?"
Rule 9) Don't ask the "Doctor" if he is still practicing medicine, or did he get it right.
Rule 10) Don't ever tell the "Doctor" it hurts when you do that to me, that will make him or her do it that much more.

So if you have the misfortune of going to one of these practitioners of medicine, just stay calm and try to maintain, which could fall under rule 11 if I went that far.

Peter Shelton

Chapter 9

We need a meeting because it has come to our attention that we are having to many meetings.

Bored? Lonely? Have a meeting! Bore your friends, impress your colleagues, and take a nap on company time. I have been witness to such bosses that give meetings for reasons just like this. This person makes an astronomical amount of money but still wants you to sit in a meeting with ten other saps. They want you to be "brought up to speed on current issues." It is to make you aware of problems that they have no intention of fixing. The best one I have ever heard was a M.L.C. meeting. That means misery loves company. Maybe it might be constructive, just maybe. Nah, they just want a nap. Instead of calling it a company meeting, they should call it nappy time. Board meetings are worse. They fly you out of state or the country to sleep (paid for by the company). They then subject them to the beach, or Hawaii, or sometimes even worse, ski trips, horse back riding, nature hikes. Where will this madness end for these poor mistreated bosses? You can see the pain in their eyes as they put the sunburn cream on their noses and comb through their sun-bleached hair. Then they tell you how rough the "Meeting" was. Real managers have a meeting once a month or so, and they talk about real issues. They do not sit there and discuss how bad the sun is for their Cancun trip. But unlike those real types of meetings, Bosses' meetings consist of sitting in an air-conditioned room with lots of soda and snacks or food, on their butts discussing what part of the world they should fly to for their next meeting. Meanwhile, you are asking your spouse if you have the money to rent a movie and get some beer. Amazing isn't it? This person can look you square in the eye (with their perfect white capped teeth) and say, "I'm sorry. It is not in our budget to give you a raise" while you say to yourself, I guess not. It went to buy the extra fuel for the plane to fly your fat ass all over the country to have a meeting. But what do I know, right? Well, I am smart enough to know that I don't need to spend three hours to discuss what food for the next meeting we would need. I was in on one once, and yes, that did come up. For one hour we discussed what they were going to eat. I don't know. I just don't get it, I guess. If I am lucky, I hope I never will if it means I will turn out like that.

With the kind of bosses we have been talking about in this book, we all know what goes on in these meetings anyway. The subject is "Who can we cut to save expenses," or "What piece of equipment can we do without," or "What benefit can we get rid of to cut expenses without touching our own," and well, you get it. Why have a meeting? I'll tell you why. They want to impress the other bosses with their sharp knowledge of how to screw the blue-collar person.

Now before you tune me out, hear me out. How many situations have you heard of that the upper bosses get these million dollar raises just after they laid a bunch of people off? How many times have you seen in the paper that the stocks go up and up, and they have another lay off? Where did the money go? Where else? It went to the boss's pocket. Owners should make money and should get all the benefits; they took the risk of having a company. But to do it on the backs of their employees is just plain wrong. They are the ones who did the work, not the bosses.

We used to have a "warehouse police person," as we called them, whose only job was to watch for people to beat time just so they could fire them. You see when someone gets fired or laid off, all that money goes to the bottom line. You get paid a lot more than what your paycheck shows between benefits and unemployment and such. So if you think you're making $10.00 an hour, you are really making about $13.00 an hour. You may think your company pays it, but with intelligent paper shuffling, you really pay it. So if you get fired or laid off, all that money goes to the bottom line, and it shows as a better outcome for that quarter and that year. Like I said early in this chapter, I had a chance to sit in on a meeting. They didn't think I had enough brains to understand what they were talking about. So they were outspoken about a lot of things.

All I learned about meetings is they don't mean much. When true managers have meetings then you have a 95 % chance to get things done the right way, but if you get bosses together, look out. Hang on to your wallet. One idea in this one meeting was that if a light bulb blew out over your work station then you must have abused it too much, and the expense should come out of your pocket because we have calculated how many hours light bulbs last. That's why we buy this kind." Yeah, I am not kidding. Here are a few more that I heard (and laughed about).

"You will wear a dollar bill on your vest (or shirt), and if you don't smile at each and every customer, they can take that dollar from you, and at the end of the week if you lost 5 dollars then you get written up."
(They can supply you with 5 dollars but can't give you a raise.)

"At lunch you must eat in the building and not go anywhere else. We need to keep track of you at all times."
(Hmmm. This is your lunch time, your time, not theirs. Why should they keep track of you? You're not getting paid through lunch.)

"On your break time do not use the restrooms; they are being cleaned."
(This one didn't fly either. In addition, this was a real thing the brain children came up with at their meetings.)

"If you have an accident and get hurt, you may be liable for damaging company equipment."

They were referring to you, not the machine. This place thought that if they considered you, a person, company property, the accidents would stop because you wouldn't want to get fired for hurting it. Don't ask me; I just write them down, but this was a real rule. I guess if I was hit in the nuts from a loose piece of machinery, I could be fired for damaging the company jewels???? Like I said, I didn't make these up, folks, I just write them down. All sorts of things come out of company meetings like these few examples.
They also came up with bosses' new and improved math in these types of meetings. The bosses' new math goes something like this. If two workers can get three boxes moved in three minutes then one worker should move two boxes in 2 minutes, so we don't need

the other worker. They will be afraid of losing his or her job so they will work faster. Bosses' new math. Another example of bosses' new math is you are short handed and can't get all your work done so you lose a few customers. The boss then lays off one or two people. Even more work gets behind, and you lose a few more customers. Again the boss lays off one or two people. Instead of hiring in the beginning so the work gets done, these idiots think lay-offs are the answer. Then you come into work one day and the place is closed. We talked about the Bosses' language; now we are going to talk about the Bosses' new math for corporate world. Another example is "If we fire three people that will be a bigger bonus at the end of the year for having less people on the payroll so that the bottom line looks better." No benefits or payroll for those people. Never mind that only half the work is going to get done. Just trim back the people. I never understood this one. For example, you are at a store. They have 15 checkout lines, and it is a really busy day. Only three checkouts are open. Why have the other 12 checkouts? They like to tease us. If they make you think that if the line gets too much longer, they will open another check out. But do they? Nooo. Only 2 out of 10 times do they. And do you know why? Because they have cut back so much that there is no one there to man them. How many times have you heard this line…"We are sorry for the wait. We are short-handed today." My reply is always "well, then tell your manager or boss to hire someone." I never get mad or ignorant with the person I am talking to because they are a peon like me.

How many times have you played telephone tag with places because they are away from the desk, have too many calls before you, or are just too busy at the time you need to speak with them? I hate, let me repeat myself I HATE, voice mail. I think Satan invented it to torture everyone. You hear that little message: "I'm sorry. I am not at my desk right now. Please leave a message after the beep, and I'll get back to you." But they never do except when you're in the bathroom or taking a shower, then they let it ring 3 or 4 times and hang up, and say well I tried. Must have been another wonderful idea that was birthed from the womb of a boss's brain. You don't have time to gab on the phone; get voice mail so that you can answer calls and get messages at the same time. That way you will always be busy. This

ties in with Bosses' new math for the corporate world. If you have
voice mail and can answer telephones, you never miss an order. You
just call them back. You can do twice as much for the same amount of
money, and at the same time, our company looks professional for
having such wonderful telephones systems.

Now I look at it like this. A company that has that god-awful
voice mail is not professional; it is cheap! I want to talk to a live
person not an answering machine. I think more of a company that has
live people in it then that stupid voice system because they think
enough of the customer to know that is what people want, someone
who can answer their questions. The only other thing worse then
voice mail is that voice menu, you know press 1 for this or press 2 for
that or press 3 for I'm going insane with this voice system. If I
wanted to play a melody with my telephone, I would buy a musical
keyboard. But we are subjected to press this for this and this for that. I
think it is another way that bosses get out of talking to customers.
You will be in telephone hell, never to see the party to whom you
want to see. This was another idea that was spurred in those meetings
of how to get out of dealing with people. Just ignore them with the
voice menu and by the time they really get to you, it is quitting time!
So I have a real low opinion of company meetings. Nothing good
ever comes out of one of those other than you don't see your boss for
a few days. So the next time your boss has a meeting just like this, it
could mean anything or go anywhere. You never know what may
come out of them, and believe me, it could be anything.

What to do when your boss tells you that a meeting is going to
happen:

1) Plan upon long weeks of fixing whatever it is they dream up.
2) Look into unemployment.
3) Look into another job.
4) See if you can't talk them into postponing it until you're on
   vacation.
5) Ask them if they need a pillow.
6) Ask them if you can sit in on the meeting; you need a good
   laugh.

7) Ask them after the meeting if they are caught up on their sleep now.
8) Ask them if they are going to tell everyone what happened or will everyone find out the day after the plant closes.
9) Ask them who got the raise this time in the meeting.
10) (This one will really blow their mind) Ask them if they remember anything that was said or done in the meeting.
11) (Say this one while eating your luncheon meat lunch) Who catered the meeting this time?
12) Ask them if they decided on where to have the corporate meeting this time: California or Florida?
13) Ask them how the Champagne was.
14) Ask them if they achieved world peace.
15) Ask them if world hunger is now solved.

Any of these will be more than enough to set them off if you have a boss. Now if you have a manager, they will understand and laugh along with you.

Chapter 10

Who is driving the bus?

The bus driver is a boss that thinks highly of himself. So highly, in fact, that without them, the company would be without direction or worse, out of business. These are the people that invented that new corporate math in one of those meetings. Even though this company has been in business for 75 years or more, it would be belly up without this person's insight. I had such a boss, a person with no clue who thought they knew everything about everything. I do mean they knew everything about everything. I have been told by this person that they were a mechanic, an electrician, a carpenter, a computer programmer, and not to forget, they had expertise at medical, manufacturing, family, stress related problems, and so on and so on.

So if this was all true, why is this dolt working here? They should be in Congress, or on a hill guru-style, answering questions that have been on society's mind for decades. Instead this person is above you like the sword of Damocles waiting for you to mess up, or asking you questions like "Is that broken?" They walk around like this is heaven, and they are god. "The bus driver" has a unusual sense of direction. Well, he really has none, but he wants you to believe he knows what he is doing like the quote, "Not to worry. I am in charge." My boss said such intelligent statements like, "There is only one bus driver here, and I'm it." Yes, he really said that just like that. A bus driver is a person, in my opinion, is not safe with his or her own sexuality, or even that of his or her own species. They act like a dog that swaggers around like they know something and are trying to prove it and hump the air (not kidding, my old boss would mark his spot if he could) trying to prove a point as lame as it might be. They try vigorously to do something but always falls short. This type of drizzling chin morons think that all things should be made in their image or done their way. Trust me, I had "A bus driver" twice, and that is how they act to a tee.

Peter Shelton

You may ask, "who does drive the bus?" My answer is no one does in a real company and with a real manager. There may be a driving force behind the business like an owner or a manager but no one bus driver. To make a company successful you need teamwork. That's from both the management and from the employees. Everyone who works at their job knows what must be done and how to do it; they for the most part don't need a bus driver over their shoulder telling them they did it wrong because they didn't do it exactly their way. Let me compare "A bus driver" to something else to show you what I mean. Ever tell a vending machine that it gave you the wrong change? Ever tell an answering machine that you know that someone is home and pick up the telephone? Talking to a bus driver is the same thing. It does no good whatsoever. You know the sad part is that I have had bosses just like I have made fun of in this book. That is why I have written it to show that I am a good sport and to poke a little fun at bosses.

So the next time you are confronted with "A bus driver" type of boss that has no idea of what he or she is doing but are trying to convince you that they do, here are some things you can do or say that will give you a little smile and them indigestion.

Statement: I am the one in charge here!

1) So you're the captain of this sinking ship.
2) I wouldn't say that too loudly if I were you.
3) You are really going to admit to that?
4) I guess you are where the crap all starts to roll downhill from.
5) Mr. Anal retentive himself.
6) The head nut?
7) You're right. You're in charge. I don't want to be held responsible for all this.
8) Could have fooled me.
9) Yeah, right.
10) How can that be? You can't find your ass with both hands.
11) Well that makes me feel better. NOT.
12) I can't believe you admitted that in front of people.

13) So you're the person I have been blaming all this time.
14) No wonder we are in such sad shape.
15) So what, so was the captain of Titanic.

Any here will give your boss the indigestion I mentioned before.

Moving on to the next type is the fickle type of bus driver. This one is a trip; they could have a three-way stop and take every one of them one at a time and still not know which way they want to go, but still maintain that they are in charge. My wonderful wife (who without her this book wouldn't have been written) (P.S. there's your plug honey) had a boss that was like this. This person would change prices on items 10 times a month. My wife had stickers upon stickers of different prices for the month.

She kept a few boxes with all the stickers just to see how many times that they would change it. It went up and down like a roller coaster. It went to 10 to 15 times a month and only by a few cents, up and down and up and down. Now instead of doing real work, they had her changing prices almost daily. So the reason the other work wasn't done was that she was too busy playing the price change game. I could understand if it changed three or four or even 5 times a month, but 10 to 15 times a month? Give me a break. That's just to see if they can get more for the product. Then it would stay at a higher price if they could get it. A fickle type of boss is the type that would have you start 3 different projects at the same time and never tell you which of the three he wants done first mainly because he doesn't know and doesn't want to tell you a wrong answer. He is also the one to sell you down the river the fastest when a major problem comes up. "Don't look at me. It's all his or her fault." In addition, if you ask them what they want to do, the answer is "Everything I need done and more!" Therefore, I made it a policy never to ask; it only gives me a headache. This type of boss, like I said, still wants to be in charge but doesn't know what to do first or how to do it. They run around like their ass is on fire and don't know where the water is. They do things 2 and 3 times or more before they decide on what they want, and then it still may change anyway. However, they still want you to know that they are in charge, and no one else. That is until the crap rolls down hill. It is a whole other ball game then.

Bosses like this are more common in places that have many different things going on like a hardware store or a department store. They are still just as nasty as the other types of bus drivers, just in a different way. The other type of bus driver is the kind that spews out the fact that they are in charge and they don't care who knows it. These types want you to know they are in charge but only when no one is around to hear it. If the owner is around or the main boss, they keep a low profile, or they kiss a lot of rump so that the main people can see what is really going on. But when in reality they haven't got a clue.

I had one such boss that really and truly asked me if he was right and I was wrong, could he assault me in a sexual manner just to punish me. (This is a family book so I left out the vulgarity.) And no, this is not an exaggeration at all (although I wish it were). These types of bosses I could really live without. To give you a more decent and not so graphic idea of this kind of boss, my whole company was once fired for 3 days and didn't even know it. Let me elaborate. On May 26th we were all told that another company was buying our company out. This was on Wednesday. On that Friday we all had to fill out applications and take a drug test. On June 9th we were all told that we had all been terminated on June 6th and had been rehired on June 7th. Now let me see. For three days we didn't know that we had been fired and rehired and didn't have insurance. Now you all are saying, and I can hear you, "well I would just call the F.L.R.B. or someone else and report them." Well, you would be wrong. The F.L.R.B. will not step in on this at all. They, the company, has the right to do anything to you they want basically. So bend over and grab your ankles, and read on. We have a way to go yet.

The way I handled it was like this. I found another job on the vacation I had left, that they thought they were being so nice giving to me even though I had earned it, and was told that it would not change. The letter I wrote went something like this:

To whom it may concern,

This is my letter of resignation. I am showing you the same courtesy that I was shown. I was terminated on June 6th, a Sunday and was notified on June 8th, so I quit on June 13th, a Sunday, and notifying you today June 16th. I wish you all the best of luck, and I did enjoy my years at (name of company), but now (name of company) is gone and so am I.

Pete Shelton
Former Proud (name of company) employee.

As you may guess this letter caused quite a stir. I had three bosses call me at home and try to bitch me out. I was told that this would go on my permanent record. I asked, what record? After all the other company bought the inventory and the customer base but not the building. It was all to be moved 25 miles away from where it was. I told them all my records show this address and all my letters of recommendation show this address so what record I have was defunct. I was then told of another big company that had lots of layoffs and they tried to compare this to that. Well the other company gave 25 weeks of severance pay and a month's notice and retraining. I, like the rest of the people that worked there, received nothing. So how did it compare? I was hung up on.

Oh, well, these things happen when you have the displeasure of dealing with a boss. All I can say is take it with a grain of salt and try not to show them anything bothers you. Otherwise, they will use it against you. You must have the upper hand here. Like me, use humor to deal with these morons that try to take away your self-esteem. I do, and it works better than yelling!

Peter Shelton

Chapter 11

"With 17 bosses you should have something to do even at the same time you do everything else!"

I love this chapter. I worked at a company that had two claim managers, three office managers, five sales managers, three computer managers, two treasurers, three vice-presidents, and one president. Now this is at a company that had a total of 18 employees. All of the above bosses had a salary above $50,000 a year plus quarterly bonuses. Now all these overpaid idiots had their own way of doing things and made sure you knew their way. And this is not, I repeat, not an exaggeration of how many bosses we had at all. They ran around like chickens with their heads cut off, and no matter what you were doing or did, you could not appease any of them. (But when all else fails, the head bus driver is always right.) So what do you do when you have ten different directions to go and all at the same time? Well, I asked one boss once. I was told, "Do it all. It should only take a hour or so to do it." In theory this sounds ok, but here is an example. How can you load one truck and unload two others and fill orders and sweep the floor all at the same time and get it done in an hour? You see these knuckle-dragging low brows think you are a robot. And isn't it strange when they fall behind, they get temps in to help them. So here you are: 17 bosses, and they all want you to go a different direction at the same time. What do you do? How can you get it all done and make these people happy without killing yourself?

The answer is you can't! You'll get old quick. Let's say you do get it all done then they expect that pace all the time and judge other employees by you. Would you or could you keep that pace up all the time? The minute you couldn't, you would get let go. You have to look at it like this: someday you'll get older. Yes, I said it. We all get old, and won't be able to work like that. What then are you going to do? Or you'll burn out and quit, and the next person will be expected to work like that. I am not saying not to work hard, but don't kill yourself for these people. They don't care. Just like a talk show host always says, "the company doesn't owe you anything; they are

there to make money." I say fine to that, then I don't owe them
either. I earn my money. They don't just give it to me so screw them.
I don't rush when I work either. I would make mistakes and that
would be worse. I would rather do the job well the first time than have
to do it again and again. No better feeling than a job well done the
first time. But having a boss like the ones I have been talking about, it
doesn't matter how well you do anything. Whatever you do, they
always want more, and that's a fact. So the next time you have two or
more bosses breathing down your neck like a vampire, here are some
quick replies say to them.

Statement: "I want you to do this…"

Even more answers…

1) Sorry, that cuts into my naptime.
2) Okay, but only if you can move time back to 6:00 A.M. so I
   can get done.
3) Break time
4) With me doing all of this, what's everyone going to do, watch
   me work?
5) Your arm's broken?
6) I would, but I have a headache.
7) Just say O.K. He'll believe you and walk away.
8) Look, I am just one person. I am doing the best I can. I am
   trying (start crying) my best. I just can't do everything… And
   so on.
9) Just start laughing and walk away.
10) I want a life so what.
11) O.k. I have two hands and two feet.
12) But your boss wants me to do this. (This will confuse them for
    a while.)
13) Just as soon as I get finished mopping the parking lot.
14) Look, Einstein, how can I get that done when I am doing all
    the other work everyone else doesn't want to do?
15) And I want a raise for doing the work of two people. What's
    your point?

Any of these answers may not put a smile on your boss's face, but it will sure make you feel better.

Ok now on to the subject of more than one boss with another way of looking at it. To give you an idea of more than one boss at any given time, think of it like this: imagine being pulled from both arms from two kids. Then add to it having your spouse on your leg and your pet pulling on your other leg all at the same time. The kids need dinner, the dog needs to go out, your spouse needs some other thing, and all are asking and pulling at you. Well, having more than one boss is much like that, only worse. They all are like overgrown kids and have the same kind of temperament. These bosses remind me a lot of kids when they act like that. Bosses forget that employees are people also and not robots.

What's worse is they don't care. Managers worry about bottom line profit, granted, but they also know to get better workers, you must act like a human being. Managers know that a happy employee is a productive employee. A lot of bosses try the scare technique, which doesn't work for me at all. They figure if they threaten to fire you every day that will increase your productivity. It does somewhat, but in the long run you get tired of hearing it and don't care anymore. So when they tell me that they are going to fire me I just kind of shrug my shoulders and smile. You would think that the buffoons would have a clue about how to be a manager, but what am I saying is that without these brainchildren, I wouldn't have a book about them all. After all, it takes all kinds (some kinds we could do without, but that's another book later). Bosses have always made me have a belly laugh when they threaten to fire me. I look at it like this I was looking for a job when I fell into this one, and I will find another one if I have to, so threaten me all you want.

I know why they do it. It is a power play. They want you to know that they can do with you whatever they want and whenever they want. They must have had overbearing parents because now they are in charge, and they want to subject you to all the years they had the thumb on them. Be that as it may, you have not one, not two, but three or more bosses like this hovering above you like vultures, and all are threatening to fire you at the same time. Trust me, it happens. I have been there. None of them really know what is going on except what's in their own little world. The outside world scares them; other bosses' wants or needs don't matter. The other boss may outrank them, but no matter, you do what I say first or else. It never ceases to amaze me how these bosses' befuddled brains work. You would need to revert 100 years to figure them out. I had a boss tell me and three other people I am the one in charge here, and about that time the other boss walks up. What happens? They get into a big fight over who is over who. We all left to let them figure it out because if they didn't know, we weren't going to tell them. And, of course, I don't think they ever got it straight, and if they did, they never told us. So the next time a boss threatens to fire you just because they can, here are some things you can tell them back that may once again prove to them that they should be flipping somewhere instead of being in charge.

"I am going to fire someone if this doesn't get done."

15 answers that may get you fired with a smile.

1) Does that mean I won't get my Christmas bonus?
2) Do me a favor. Do it now so I can get to the unemployment office before the lunch crowd.
3) OOOOO Hurt my feelings.
4) Then who is going to get it done? You don't make me laugh.
5) So, I was looking for a job when I got trapped into this one.
6) OOOOOOOO I am so scared.
7) You trying to get me excited or what?
8) Bite me.
9) Fall on your knees and say, "Thank you. Thank you."
10) Then who would you blame because it didn't get done?
11) Too bad your boss didn't tell you that.
12) Ya know a month ago that would have bothered me, but I now know how low the intelligence level is you have, and I don't think you could fill out the paperwork, and even if you could, so what.
13) Well thank you for trying to brighten up my day.

14) Well that's a surprise.
15) Well if you fire me, that means you might have to do it, and I don't think you're smart enough. Besides, it has been so long since you have done real work, I don't think you would remember how to work.

Any of these answers will get the reaction you might be looking for. And always remember, smile when you talk to a boss. Never, as a rule, yell at them. When you start yelling or name-calling, they win, and that's what they want. Always keep a cool head, and you always come out ahead of the game.

Now the last chapters of this book are kind of short. I have a reason for that. I am by no means running out of material if that is what you are thinking. I decided to keep this book short and humorous, and if I go too wild on the last few chapters, it would lose some of the feel of the book. So I figured to keep the end kind of short and sweet. Like the old saying goes, leave them wanting more. So don't be surprised to have the last chapters short and sweet.

Peter Shelton

Chapter 12

Suggestions for the suggestions box

We all have one, or at least we all know that bosses always want, or at least they say they want to hear them. But when it comes down to real life they don't want to hear from you. They tell you that to make you feel like you may have an idea that might be a little halfway good…maybe. And if it is a good idea, they will just tell the head boss "Yes, like MY idea sir?" "Aren't I wonderful? Aren't I a great thinker?" And so on and so on. Their brains have given up trying to get a new thought or idea in that stack of cobwebs a long time ago so they use everyone else's. These bosses hang these things in one or two places:

A: Over a trash bin.
B: Over their office so they can either screen or use them for themselves.

Now again we are not talking about managers here just bosses. A manager will give credit where credit is due. I know I always come back and compare bosses to managers, but I want to be sure everyone is clear on this point. Managers are good bosses, and a "Boss" and a manager are two different animals all together. Anyway a suggestion box is, like I said, used two different ways, and bosses who have these things have no ideas left so they need help wherever they can find it. I love it. They don't want free thinkers, but they want their ideas in Suggestion boxes. Free thinkers are the people that build computers and write books and write music. In the world of employment and Bosses, however, free thinkers are dangerous and need to be tamed down for "the good of the company."

Well I have a few suggestions for them as you might have guessed, and I use them as often as I can. I always get credit for them also, but I want the recognition that goes with my suggestions. When these boxes of evil come forth and get hung on the wall, the only thing you can do about it is go with it. Put lots of suggestions in them, anything you want or would like to see, even if you just want to be a "Smart ass" like a few chapters ago and just want somewhere to vent. After all you don't have to sign your name if you don't want to. Well here is the prime place to do it. Trust me, I did it enough. And if some boss that has their head in a place that should never have a head in it (and you know what I mean) and hangs one of the treasures up, here are but a few ideas that might give you some suggestions for your box at work.

Suggestions for the Suggestion box!

1) Fire all the bosses.
2) Give everyone a raise so we can be at minimum wage.
3) Stop having meetings and find out what is really going on with your company.
4) Have equipment that is newer and isn't from the turn of the century.
5) Suggest that all the bosses go and have a mental exam.
6) Suggest that the bosses should find a new line of work; you don't care where or what, just somewhere else.
7) Suggest that the upper bosses stop skimming off the top profits so the other people who work there might get a raise once in a while.
8) Suggest that they take a course in management training to learn what they have been doing wrong all these years.
9) Suggest that they have real incentives for a change.
10) Suggest that the management look into straight jackets because in your opinion they're all nuts.
11) Suggest that management take a long holiday so the employees can get more work done.
12) Print your suggestion on a picture with a nude person with a note saying, "Just wanted to see if you really pay attention to these suggestions."
13) Tell them you would put a suggestion in the box, but you didn't think by the way they do things they were smart enough to read it.

14) Write your suggestion on toilet paper. Since you act like your head is stuck up your ass anyway, maybe written on toilet paper you might just read it.
15) Write your suggestion and misspell all the words really off the wall. He will spend all day trying to figure it out.

They really didn't want your ideas anyway. They just wanted to make you feel like you had some sort of control over what is going on at your workplace. It is an old trick, but that is one of many ways to fight the suggestion box. There are a few others I will mention here:

* Hide the box, and let it show up everyday in a different spot. Make sure the boss is the one who finds it first.
* Put another lid on it without an opening for the envelope hole.
* Paint it different colors.
* Hang it upside-down.
* Hang out-of-order signs on it.
* Put it outside by the boss's car.
* Write long, and I mean long, letters to it everyday. Sooner or later they will get tired of unloading it.

Like I said, there are a few other ways to combat the box. And of course out of the box other forms of ideas spawn, or maybe because of them. Ever have a quality control meeting? Those kinds of meetings should be called the money meeting. It really means instead of quality control they are worried about bottom line and Money. Yep, there are those phrases again. Amazing how they pop up a lot when dealing with bosses. I said it once and I'll say it again, we all agree that companies need to make profit otherwise why be in business? How much is enough? And why should money be the deciding factor in whether or not to get the ladder fixed so someone won't fall and get hurt?

I mean common sense should have some say in the wonderful world of work. And I'll also remind you that all of these stories are true in this book, and that's what makes them so funny and so scary at the same time.

But back to the lighter side – the quality control meeting. This is a different kind of meeting all together, not like a sleepy time meeting, or "I want to hear myself brag" meeting; this is a whole other kind of animal. This one deals mainly with money. Any and all forms of money. They don't care where they save the money, just save and make more. But at the same time they want other people to do it for them. Typical corporate thinking. They want to increase the quality which I can understand but at the same time at what cost? I used to drive a truck and delivered to a place that had this sign hung up. It read, and I am quoting it to the letter, "All orders will be filled on time correctly and without any excuse. NO exceptions." Well that's all good and well, but you know they didn't even allow for human error or machines breaking down, and I have seen them fire the whole line when that happens. From what I understand, this was birthed from one of those quality control meetings. Imagine retraining 20 or so people every 8 to 9 months. Waste more money in re-training than they save, but if you ask the brainchildren who are in charge, they tell me differently. Shows you how smart they really are.

I didn't say I understand them, but this is what came out of their mouths. Anyway that is one of many things that come out of quality control meetings. Another brother of the suggestion box is the voice message idea line. I don't know how popular this is around the country, but I have been at a few spots that this idea was in place. The way it works is like this: you have an idea, you want to voice your idea, you call a number, talk into this messaging system, and it records your idea. This kind of suggestion box is typical at larger companies where the main office is based out of town, like if you worked in Missouri and the corporate office is in Texas. That way if it is a good idea they may use it on all of their locations. This suggestion has a few major flaws. For one if the idea would be of use at your location, you may never know unless they did it if it was lost in voice mail hell. Two, it may get erased a lot easier by "mistake." Three, no one really has to answer questions like, "What did you think of my idea"? Four, no one will really know where the idea ever came from and so no one but the upper management gets the credit for it. Well you know I hate voice mail to start. I mean everyone has called and gotten that damn machine with that message, "Please leave a brief

message after the beep." If you are at a business, you should answer
you own phone. It is a sign of courtesy. I go out of my way to mess
with voice systems. Even when you are trying to reach your boss for
some reason, let's say, and they are out to lunch or getting their 18th
trip to the water cooler, or trying to impress the secretary. I savor the
chance to leave a voice message. Some of the things I do and say
which you may want to try are as follows, but remember don't give
any names when you use these.

Order a pizza.
Make rude noises.
Ask for the time and temp.
Ask for a phone number and wait until it beeps. (This will use up all
of the room on the voice message system.)
Ask for directions.
Read out of the newspaper.
Talk to it as if you're from another country and don't speak English.
(Just make up some gibberish and start talking)
Act like this is a 911 call, and no one is answering.
Act like this is the number your boy or girlfriend or spouse gave you
to the person they are cheating with.
Ask them if this is the suicide hotline, and again ask why no one is
answering.

These are just a few lines that you can use on these machines.
The funny part is that the bosses will never notice the different. I
think they use these machines because they don't want to deal with
real people. I once saw a cartoon that said it all. It had a boss behind
a desk with a big cigar and an employee standing in front of him
pointing at a sign. The sign read, "We care about people." The boss
told the employee, "You're not people you jerk, you work here."
Ain't it the truth! You know managers rely on their people to help
them because without the job the employee would not have a job to
start with, but bosses don't care about people. All they look at is…can
we all say it now, "BOTTOM LINE". That's why voice mail came
into play. Why have someone to answer a phone and take messages
when a cheap machine or a program on a computer can do it for

almost nothing? I have known managers that refuse to get voice mail for two reasons; one of which is because computers and machines sometimes mess up, then what do you do if it was an important message. The other reason is because a real person will take a written message, and also it is nice to talk to a real person on the phone rather than a voice-generated recording. We used to play phone tag at one of my jobs. We had to call in when we were sick, of course. No one wanted to talk to a boss and hear that OLE line, "well we really need you here today." So when we got the voice mail, we all got up even earlier just so we didn't have to talk to a boss. We would just leave a message. I myself had a computer so I used to fax them to let them know I wasn't coming and also had proof that I did notify them of my absence, I would bring in the fax statement. So I guess that these machines weren't all that bad, after it got me out of talking to my boss when I didn't want to anyway.

Chapter 13

You can always talk to me; my door is always open.

Yeah right! We're talking about the same kind of employees in this book as always, the "Low Brain Activity" type. They don't want to hear from you or even care because if they really do then you're reading the wrong book. If the bosses did care, count your blessings and go buy him or her card. And as always I am talking about the bosses, not managers. So as I was saying, they don't care and don't want to talk to you. They are too busy asking dumb questions. All they want are robots with no problems or concerns. Their door is not always open; it just appears to be. It is really a locked door (a massive deadbolt) from the inside with a picture of an open door painted on it. The "Open Door" policy is really a myth and an extinct type of theory.

Open door means the boss's door is open all right but so is their back door which leads to the outside. You go into one open door and leave the building through the other open door. The first door slams shut behind you.

Meanings for Open Door Policy:

1) Give me the ammo to fire you.
2) Tell me something that can get me promoted by demeaning you or someone else.
3) Give me an idea that I can take credit for.
4) Tell me your secrets so I can laugh and tell everyone else.
5) Tell me anything that I can use against you or someone else.
6) Last but not least tell me something I can use to make myself feel better.

Now not all bosses do this, but a lot of the winners I have run into have. You know by reading this far into this book and about me and the bosses I have had, you would think that I have some damn bad jobs. Well, I have not had bad jobs, just bad bosses. Anyway I thought I should throw that in here real quick. Moving on the "Open Door Policy" isn't all that it is cracked up to be. It's another way the bosses get their jollies and to intimidate their employees. These kinds of bosses are the kind that when you walk away from them and have your back to them, look out for that sign they'll hang on your back that says kick me. Or that knife they'll stick into you back when your head is turned. Now in the good old days (remember those) an Open Door Policy meant just that. You could talk with your boss without fear of reprimand or anything else. Now that corporate and the corporate mind-set, you just never know what might happen if you even say hi to them in the wrong way. As I talked about earlier, the handbooks they come up with and the guidelines set forth by companies are really funny, and I will go through a few of them here.

First and foremost, since it is the name of the chapter, is the "Open Door Policy." Now this was in the manager handbook that was shown to me by a fellow employee so that I might use it in this book, so I will. These may sound like the other six I mentioned, but the difference is that these are right out of a handbook. The other six were just what I thought the policy meant, and as always I explained what they really mean in parentheses.

The "Open Door Policy" here at (company's name) should be treated and viewed as six different things:

1) As a way to get to know the employee better on a whole, a happy employee is a better worker. (Like they really want to know who you are)

2) As a way to let employees to vent their frustrations about they're working environment. (They won't do anything about it, but you can bitch at them about it)

3) As a way that we can find out where the problems are and can address them. (Which means they will have someone to blame.)

4) As a way to find out how the employees understand their duties. (Which means some of the things they want you to do must be so damn complicated or stupid that it takes a week to figure out how to do, whatever it is they are asking you to do.)

5) As a way to help with the employees if they have any problems that might interfere with their duties. (This means what kind of dirt they can get on you to either hold it over your head or fire you with now.)
6) As a way to find out about fellow employees if there are any internal conflicts that must be addressed. (And this means who else they can find out about to hold something over their head or fire them.

But I am sure that if you have read this far you might know that there are a few ways to combat this also. The "Open Door Policy" is neither a hard one to figure out nor a hard one to overcome. Just for starters use common sense and a quick wit whenever talking to a boss. If for some strange reason you decide to go to one of these open doors to hell, always remember that whatever you say can and will be used against you.

Remark: You can always talk to me. My door is always open.

Here are some answers for the boss that should let him know how you feel.

1) Just like your mouth.
2) Is that where all the screaming is coming from?
3) Too bad your mind is not as open.
4) Just what I need, another place where I can get yelled at without witnesses.
5) Kind of like a bathroom stall in a men's room.
6) Close it and quit will ya.
7) Like the gates of hell?
8) That's the same thing Satan said.
9) No thanks I can't roll my pant legs up any higher than this.
10) What for? So you can impress everyone with your new office furniture?
11) Too cheap to buy a door or what?
12) Lost the key huh…
13) You just can't figure out how to close it yet.

14) I've seen it closed. You can't fool me. It's closed every time you have your secretary (or office boy) in there.
15) Open door? Yeah, well, I think not. I have a place to go that's just as open, and I know it has a spot to flush.

Any of these will make your boss turn all sort of funny colors. Not all open door policies are bad. It really depends on your boss. If you have a manager then it is a good thing, but if you have a boss, all bets are off. A lot of bosses also use a "talk to me anytime" policy. I always ask them for their home phone number so that I can call them at three in the morning. I never get it, but I ask. Hey if they are going to say it, I am going to use it. When dealing with an "Open Door Policy" or any of its spawned offspring, use everything you can think of if you have a boss.

Chapter 14

How to give notice and leave a smile on your face and a frown on their's.

Well here we go into the last of this and the most important part of this book…
HOW TO QUIT!
Yes that's right. There is a right way to quit a job with a boss and one with a manager. You know a boss never gives you the right kind of notice or warning when they lay you off or when they fire you. You come in one day, and that's it. No warning like hey we may have cut backs, or you had better shape up or you're out. I was at one place that told this lady she was the greatest thing since sliced bread all the way up until they fired her. The reason they kept her was because she wore short skirts. Then one day she was "Let go" not really even knowing why she was let go. She had been there six months and was being told she was doing well until she got married. You can figure out the rest. Nice, huh? What a wonderful place that was to work for. I asked if I wore short pants if they would give me a promotion, but that didn't work. Another guy I knew from a different job was let go the day back from his vacation. The company I worked at was sold, and they put a BOSS in charge of an 80 million-dollar a year plant, which by the way, he ran out of business in less than five years. Anyway, he was put in charge, and this man had worked for this company for 20 years, but this boss didn't like him. So this man went on vacation, and the day he got back, they told him to get out. He asked if he could clean out his office and was told no. They would send everything to his house. They had two other bosses clean out his personal items. The funny part was he didn't tell them of the booby traps he had in his office so that he knew he could get back at someone who rummaged though his desk when he was on vacation or gone. He had rat traps and paint bombs and all sorts of things that blew up in there. I think we all laughed all day every time we heard something pop. At this same place they told another sales manager that she had to leave the same day she told them she had a job offer.

Again they told her that they would clean out her desk for her, (she had already done that two days before, unknown to them). The only thing they found was a note that said "Kiss my A**." I would have paid money to see the look on the face on the boss's face when they read that note. For the next two days the boss was walking around with a red face. And one salesperson was told his sales were down for the last month, and if his sales didn't pick up, he would be let go. That doesn't sound too bad, but he just had a major heart attack. So I don't feel bad in the slightest for quitting the way I and others do. I do it with a smile. Or how about when we all have gotten laid off without notice? How does that make you feel? But when you quit, I always hear the same old tired thing, don't you want to give us a two-week notice or a three-week notice or even a month? Do you know how long it will take to replace you? Can you re-train the next person that we hire? Like I said, why is it that when bosses let you go for any or all reasons, they never give us notice, but they want their's. They want to know when you are leaving so that they can fire you first, and that way if it doesn't work out at the next job, they can block your unemployment. Well, I have many ways around that, and use them every chance I need to. I hold no loyalty to any employer anymore. No one should. It is, after all, just a job, not a way of life. If it starts becoming a way of life to people then they have more problems than I or anyone can fix. People should realize that a job is a means to an end, nothing more. It does not mean you should slack off or steal or something stupid, but it does mean don't take it so seriously. We have all seen people think that their job is their life and that being unemployed was almost a reason to end it all or something. All I have to say is that they should look into professional help. When a job becomes all important that nothing else matters, or your time is so consumed by work then it's time to make changes or move on to a better job. So when that time comes and you do want to move on, the way you do it is all-important. You must leave with…Style! When leaving with Style, you must always have a job to go to first. It is always easier to find a job when you have one to start with.

So when dealing with the boss and how to quit, I always say do to them what they have done to others or to you. One of the things I love to do is to re-train someone. I re-train them wrong as I can get away with it without the bosses catching on until after I leave. They can't get mad at the person I trained because they were trained this way. It just cost the company more money to re-re-train them. So giving notice isn't a problem for me. There are some people who don't want to quit a job they hate just because they don't want to face the boss and tell them. I used to be that way until I had this wonderful example of this book-type boss. I had to do things that were so far out in left field that it was unreal. Like the time he made me mop up sewer water outside then use that same mop head on the store inside after I rinsed it out. Mind you it was a restaurant. First of all, why should I have to mop up sewer water outside since the city was washing it down a manhole the next day? Second, I by no means would ever use a mop in my house no matter how many times I rinsed it out after it had been in sewer water. Of course, I never ate there again. I was 16 years old and had that much sense but not this boss. I told him use a squeegee and squeegee it down the manhole cover, and I was told I was being lazy. Hmm…let me think. I wanted to do it right, which would have taken more work instead of using a mop that we used on out floors that people eat on. I then told him that I would change the mop head and get a new one and throw this one away. Nope just wash it out unless you want to buy a new one. They aren't cheap, you know. He even tried to get me to climb up to the top of the building and change the letters on the sign. Which would not have been too bad except for the fact that I was 240lbs. at 6 foot 4, and the only thing to stand on was 2, 2 by 4 boards because the rest of the wood had rotted away, and they never fixed it. It was also 40 feet up. Of course I denied the offer for being a stunt person and quit that night. Oh well, one good thing, this place has been long gone out of business. That's the first job I quit, but it was not the last. I got used to it after having a bevy of nutty bosses with a tin god syndrome that think you should do acrobatics to make a living, or be a personal whipping post.

You learn really quickly when working for bosses which job you'll stay at for a while and which one you won't. I'll say within the first 20 minutes most of the time. Sometime it takes a few weeks but never longer than that. But when you do run into these types, never be afraid to leave and move on to greener pastures. And I know you always hear the grass is always greener on the other side until you get there. That is true too, BUT they may not be as much manure, you know what I mean?

So when looking for a job, I don't look for greener pastures so much as how much manure is around. I don't want to roll up my pant legs just to go to work. So on to how to quit with *Style*! TWO important rules you should use. Never, I repeat NEVER, tell them where you went or what job you went to. And never be destructive. Any idiot can destroy something; you have to use Style to quit.

They are many ways to do this, but I have as always 15 ways that I consider to work the best on bosses.

1) Fax them with a copy of your ass, covered or not, your choice, with a note telling them to mail your checks to you.
2) Send a singing telegram to your boss like, "This job stinks on ice so I went somewhere that treats me nice but don't think I'm funny, just send me my money."
3) After you find a job, start it and call in sick, and tell them you'll never be back. Mail your check, and you can't talk long because you're on break from you new job.
4) Plan a party telling the boss it's a birthday party or something and bring in a cake on this party with the lettering on the cake stating I QUIT.
5) If your company is able to have a radio on, call the station that your boss listens to and have it broadcast it over the air.
6) My buddy did this one. He brought in a cake in the shape of a butt, and it looked just like a butt with the vertical smile, and all with the words lettered on it KISS MY BUTT GOODBYE!
7) If your company has designated parking areas with names on it, bring in a sign that says Vacant, then go in and ask for your checks.
8) Send your boss some flowers like lilies with a note saying, "I thought this would be appropriate since you're killing the company. I am leaving for a better job before the last shovel of dirt hits me. Have a nice day."

9) I would say put it in the suggestion box, but they never read that so buy some balloons and see if you can have them write on them I QUIT! And hang them in your boss's office.

10) Fill up all the bosses' voice mail with your name and I QUIT SEND ME MY CHECKS on a loop over and over again.

11) Hand them written notice and pre-date for two weeks ago, like if you quit let's say 6/17/99, date it for 6/1/99. They won't notice and have them sign a copy, and then you have proof that you did give notice if it ever comes up somewhere.

12) Send them a postcard from somewhere exotic saying, "Having a wonderful time. Glad you're not here. Send me my last check."

13) Send them a picture of your face and a note saying this is the last you'll see of me, send me my last checks.

14) Send them some kind of weed that people have allergies to in bloom. Put it in a pot with a ribbon on the pot. Then put your "I Quit" note on it. Chances are they never notice what it is and every sneeze and bout of watery eyes will be thanks to you.

15) Come in and tell them you quit. When they start giving you that lecture about the two weeks notice thing and retraining someone and such, put in some ear plugs and sit and smile at them and nod your head, but put the plugs in front of the boss then watch them turn red.

Now this is an extra one that I always wanted to do but have never had the chance to try... YET,

16) Go into your boss's office before he gets there with a big cigar and a bottle of grape wine. Light it up and start sipping the wine. When your boss gets there, lightly flick the ashes onto his floor and say oops that may start a fire like that, let me put it out. Then pour the bottle of grape wine on the ashes on the floor. Ask the boss to sign your safety report for stopping a possible fire.

Well, that's about it for this chapter and this book. Like I said, the last of this book was going to be short and sweet. I hope that you have all read this far and have gotten a good laugh and have nodded your head in a few spots. This book is all in good fun, and I hope you have had as much fun reading it as I have had writing it. A bit of poking fun at bosses is good for them once in a while. If any bosses have read this book, I would say I hoped you have learned something, but hey, who would I be kidding? If they could change then why would I have written this book to start with. Besides I don't think most of them could have understood the bigger words in this book anyway. And if any managers have read this book, for you I have the utmost respect, and I hope that you stay that way. Nothing is better than a manager that respects their employees. Bosses are in themselves unique. They are the things that go bump in the office; they are the things that scare little children; they are the things nightmares are about. It's a shame that they let bosses breed at all, but it they weren't here, I wouldn't have a book, and there wouldn't be songs about quitting your job. There would be signs up about waiting for Friday and beer wouldn't be so expensive.

There wouldn't be people saying, "I have to get away for a weekend," because we would all live in a wonderful world with wonderful jobs and perfect managers that have brains. There would be no need for cartoons or TV shows about working. So you bosses do have a use; you're the butt of a lot of jokes, and you employ more people than you thought.

Well I am done now so I hope that you liked the book, got a few snickers and laughs, and always my number one rule that supercedes everything: Don't take life seriously. Enjoy life for it is a short time you're here, and a job is just that, a job. It's a means to an end; life is much more so enjoy it while you can.

The End

About the Author

Peter Shelton has been published in the St. Louis Post Dispatch, "Life is Precious," 1996. He was also published with a short story entitled, "My Son the Rainbow," in, <u>The Treasure of a New You</u>, book collection by Catherine Galassos. He has now taken a blue collar approach at humor with his new book, <u>The Working Persons Pocket Guide to Boss and Employees Relations or 103 Ways to Leave Your Boss Speechless</u>. Quips and witty comebacks with these hard to deal with situations. How to find humor and sanity when everyone else is getting ulcers or contemplating the bosses demise. A fun loving approach to your hemorrhoidal boss. This will definitely leave you laughing and your boss speechless.

Printed in the United States
22442LVS00006B/577